Teaching Literary Elements With Picture Books

Engaging Standards-Based Lessons and Strategies

Susan Van Zile and Mary Napoli

NEW YORK · TORONTO · LONDON · AUCKLAND · SYDNEY

MEXICO CITY · NEW DELHI · HONG KONG · BUENOS AIRES

Teaching *Resources*

Acknowledgments

This book is dedicated to the Great Creator and to the gifts in each of us that come through us but are not of us.

To my mentor, Dr. Mary Napoli, whose passion for children's books, deep knowledge, and generosity are unsurpassed.

To Virginia Dooley, Editorial Director of Scholastic Grades 4–8 Professional Books, and Terry Cooper, Editor-in-Chief of Scholastic Professional Books, for giving me the courage and opportunity to live a dream.

To my husband, daughter, son, and parents for their abiding unconditional love and support.

— Susan Van Zile

This book would not have been possible without the support of my family, friends, and colleagues. It is dedicated to our wondrous Creator for the insurmountable blessings, people, and opportunities that cross our paths.

To my friend and extraordinary educator and colleague, Susan Van Zile for sharing her passion for teaching and learning. Thank you for your unending support and inspiration. Most of all, thank you for the opportunity to work with you on this project and for inviting me to take this professional journey with you.

Finally, a special thank you to my husband, Jody Putt, my sister, Victoria Napoli, and my parents, Josephine and Patrick Napoli, for their unending support, love, and encouragement.

— Mary Napoli

To Tyler Zoellner, Jessica Pearson, Nicole Smith, Kim Barr, and Emily Ritholz for giving us permission to incorporate their lessons. To our colleagues from the National Writing Project for providing the context, tools, and inspiration to guide our journeys as writing teachers.

To our magnificent students whose imaginations, creativity, and enthusiasm inspire us, teach us, and bring us joy.

— Mary Napoli and Susan Van Zile

Cover design and illustration by Jason Robinson
Interior design by Melinda Belter
Acquiring Editor: Virginia Dooley
Editor: Sarah Glasscock
Copy Editor: Carol Ghiglieri
ISBN-13: 978-0-439-02799-1
ISBN-10: 0-439-02799-3

Contents

Introduction
What's Inside This Book and Why

In order to read critically and interpretively and "to write with stylistic awareness" (Hall, 2002, p. vii), students need to understand, interpret, and apply their knowledge of literary devices.[1] While understanding literary devices is only one component of being able to read analytically and to write richly, it is an important one. The primary purpose of this book is to introduce methods and ideas for transferring writing skills and literary devices from literature to student writing. Once students learn to recognize and interpret literary devices and understand why authors use these devices, they can incorporate these devices into their own writing (Olness, 2005).

At both the intermediate and middle school levels, picture books offer an invigorating and illuminating new dimension to the teaching of literary devices to promote student reading and writing. Immersing students in these "thirty-two page wonders" (Hall, 2002, p. ix) and inviting them to look closely at both the "writer's process and the craft of the texts" (Wood Ray & Laminack, 2001, p. 139) are extremely useful elements for developing the writer's craft. As Ralph Fletcher and Joan Portalupi (1998) note, "the writing you get out of your students can only be as good as the classroom literature that surrounds and sustains it" (p. 10). Shanahan (1990) concurs with the idea that writers are influenced by readers and readers are informed by writers:

> Readers think about authors, and writers think about readers. The fusion of reading and writing in the classroom offers students the possibility of participating in both sides of the communication process and, consequently, provides them with a more elaborate grasp of the true meaning of literacy. (pp. 4 & 11)

Thus, to become better writers and to incorporate literary devices naturally and seamlessly into their writing, students need to be exposed to quality language and rich vocabulary that outstanding selections of literature possess.

Picture books have traditionally been found only in elementary school classrooms; however, the stigma associated with integrating picture books in intermediate and middle school classrooms is fading. Many teachers have been reluctant to use picture books to support instruction, yet a majority of current picture books are particularly geared for adolescents. Many picture books are "sophisticated, abstract, or complex in themes, stories, and illustrations" (Lynch-Brown & Tomlinson, 2005, p. 83). As Frank Serafini (2007) notes in his position statement about the vital role of picture books in the intermediate classroom, "picture books support older readers as they encounter writing techniques and literary elements" (p. 1).

To accomplish our goal of having students incorporate literary devices into their writing, we read and reviewed numerous picture books before making our final selections. Moreover, we decided to focus on texts published from 2000–2007 to acquaint students and teachers with some of the excellent new books that are currently on the market. Although each book selected relates to a specific literary device, many can be used for more than one purpose. For example, we've included *Prairie Train* by Marsha Wilson Chall as a literature selection for metaphor; however, it contains exquisite imagery and extraordinary similes as well.

In addition to selecting contemporary picture books, we've also included a variety of genres. Humorous tall tales and works of nonfiction appear as well as multicultural texts, such as *Elephant Dance* by Theresa Heine and *Across the Alley* by Richard Michelson. Because of recent research related to boys and writing, including Tim Newkirk's assertion (2004) in *Misreading Masculinity* that the central genre for boys is satire and parody, we have included both of these literary elements.

The basic format of this book, with some variation, is as follows:

◆ Each lesson begins by identifying the literary device being introduced, along with its definition and an example from the selected literature.

◆ Bibliographic information and brief summaries of the selected literature and two additional literature selections appear next.

◆ Materials and reproducibles for each lesson appear in a sidebar. Only materials that may not be readily available in the classroom are listed.

◆ Then we present a detailed lesson idea specifically related to the selected literature that incorporates before-, during-, and after-reading strategies.

◆ A writing activity gives students practice with the literary device.

◆ Finally, one or more lesson extensions either extends the writing activity, include a writing idea for the other literature selections, or crosses over to other content areas.

A lesson usually begins with an activity that is designed to introduce students to the specific literary element as they listen to the selected text. Activating background knowledge is a powerful resource students use to understand text. Research indicates that students with prior knowledge of a topic retain more information than do those with little or no prior knowledge (Vacca & Vacca, 2008). Teachers can bring students and texts together by using a before-, during-, and after-reading instructional framework. Before-reading activities help to establish a purpose for reading, activate background knowledge, build motivation, and focus attention on important information. During-reading activities aim to encourage active reading and provide opportunities for students to use higher-order thinking skills. After-reading activities extend and elaborate ideas from the text.

To maximize the effectiveness of each lesson, we recommend having multiple copies of the text available; however, all lessons can be conducted with a single copy. You can also use a document camera or project the text on an overhead to enhance the lessons. Naturally, when you read aloud with expression and share the illustrations, you serve as an effective role model. Reading aloud quality literature provides the foundation for each lesson.

The writing activities invite students to incorporate the literary devices into their own writing. Some writing activities are simple scaffolds that encourage students to imitate the author. Often this scaffolding is essential if the ultimate goal, having students naturally use literary elements, is to be achieved. In fact, Peter Lancia (1997) encourages the technique of "literary borrowing," acknowledging that "as any novice learns by imitating a role model, children learn about writing by interacting with professional writers" (p. 471). Once students have enough practice using the literary element, it will become a natural part of their own writing.

Since writing is a process, some of the writing activities may take more time than others. For example, a simple scaffolding activity may take a single 40-minute class period whereas developing a script for Readers Theater may take two or three periods. In classrooms where the writing process is employed, teachers may need to differentiate instruction to accommodate the needs of their individual students.

Note that many of the lessons incorporate sample graphic organizers; some of these graphic organizers have corresponding reproducibles, while others do not. Most of the graphic organizers are easily created on chart paper or the computer, and others are readily available on the Internet; the following Web sites are excellent sources for graphic organizers:

Houghton Mifflin Education Place: http://www.eduplace.com/graphicorganizer/

Visual-Literacy: http://www.visual-literacy.org/periodic_table/periodic_table.html#

Scholastic: http://www2.scholastic.com/browse/search?query=graphic+organizers+

Finally, our ultimate hope is that this book will help you and your students select, read, and enjoy quality literature and to use it as a vehicle to promote quality writing. May these pages foster joy and delight in learning and ignite a deep passion for reading and writing in your classroom.

---

[1] Throughout this book, the terms *literary devices* and *literary elements* are used interchangeably.

Imagery/Sensory Language

Imagery creates mental pictures through sensory language—
words or phrases that appeal to the five senses.

"Every Saturday she spread a cloth over the red countertop and
scattered a fistful of flour across it, sending a cloud into the air."

from *Saturday and Teacakes* by Lester Laminack

✳ ✳ ✳

Selected Literature

Saturday and Teacakes by Lester Laminack, illustrated by Chris Soentpiet, 2004,
Peachtree Publishers

Every Saturday a young boy pedals his bike to Mammaw's house where she
waits just for him. Rich, sensory descriptions of freshly cut grass and sweet
teacakes surround this family love story.

Other Possible Literature Selections

Stranger in the Woods: A Photographic Fantasy by Carl R. Sams and Jean Stoick, 2000,
EDCO Publishing

A mysterious stranger in the forest ignites the animals' curiosity. As the forest
buzzes with conversation and stunning photographs unfold across the page, the
stranger's identity is revealed.

Dream: A Tale of Wonder, Wisdom, & Wishes by Susan V. Bosak, illustrated by Leon Dillon,
Diane Dillon, Robert R. Ingpen, and Raúl Colón, 2004, TCP Press

With color and sensory imagery infused throughout the poetic text, Bosak
explores the nature and power of dreams, the hope they inspire, and the
knowledge that acting on them can change the world.

Lesson Idea

To motivate students to attend to the imagery and sensory language in *Saturday and Teacakes*, create sensory shoe boxes. For example, in a smell box, place spices such as cinnamon and ginger in small plastic bags as well as a variety of other objects with strong scents. A sound box might include a rattle, a bell, and finger cymbals. Make taste bags for individual students with a small sampling of salty, sweet, bitter, or fruity items in them. Have groups of three or four students explore each sensory box.

After each group records words related to their sensory experiences on a chart like the one below, it exchanges a sensory box with another group.

See	Hear	Feel	Smell	Taste
shiny tin	ding	scratchy wool	like a cinnamon roll	buttery

After the charts are completed, groups do a quick group share. As one group shares its chart with another group, the listeners record any words they do not have. Remind students not to repeat any words recorded by the other group.

Before, During, and After Reading

Prior to reading *Saturday and Teacakes* aloud, ask students to share a special memory of a grandparent or relative that is sensory-rich, such as baking cookies with Gram or enjoying Thanksgiving at a relative's house.

Encourage students to attend to the sensory language as you read the story aloud to them. Model the process first: Read the first two pages of text. Then stop to think aloud about the imagery and sensory language you recall and list it on the board. Continue reading. After you finish reading the story, have students make a quick list of the images and sensory language they remember and share their lists. Write students' ideas on chart paper and post the list in the classroom so they can refer to it as they write.

Writing Activity

Ask students to write a memoir about a vivid childhood memory, using imagery and sensory language to transport the reader to that time and place. Use the following steps to help you guide students through the memoir-writing process:

1. Have students create a heart map of memories. In the center they write memories of people, places, animals, events, joys, and sorrows that are closest to their hearts. "Close to the heart" memories might include the birth of a sibling or the death of a pet. On the edges of the heart map students include memories that are not as strong, such as drinking a thick, rich milkshake on a scorching summer day. (This idea is suggested by Georgia Heard in *Awakening the Heart: Exploring Poetry in Elementary and Middle School*. For best results, model your own heart map first.)

2. Tell students to choose one memory to write about. Ask them to bring two or three objects related to that memory to class the next day, if possible.

3. Next, direct students to draw a picture of the memory. As they draw, ask nudging questions to help them add detail. (Use the Teacher's Script for Memoir-Nudging Questions reproducible.)

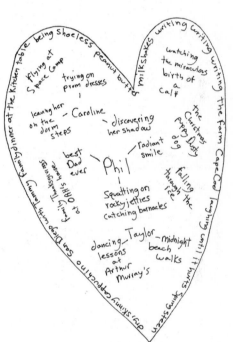

A completed heart map of memories

4. After drawings are complete, pair students and send them on a partner walk and talk. Designate a walking route and specify the exact location where partners should switch roles from speaker to listener and vice versa. As students walk, they should take turns telling each other as much as they can about their drawings. Emphasize that speakers should not stop talking until they reach the halfway point.

   If they run out of things to say before they are halfway through the walk, their partner must ask them questions about their memory. Model a few questions for them. For example, if a student describes a nighttime beach walk, his partner might ask, "What kind of sea creatures did you see on your walk?"

5. After the partner walk and talk, ask students to complete a Memoir Map reproducible before drafting their memoir.

6. Have students peer edit the drafts. The peer editor should highlight the images and sensory language and think about how the writer can create a more vivid picture for the reader. Ask peer editors to make suggestions about what the writer can add, delete, move, or substitute to improve the memoir.

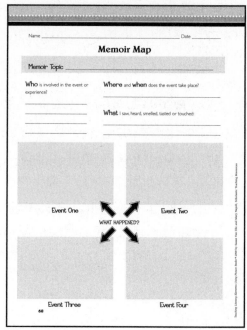

Memoir Map

7. Finally, ask students to write a final copy based on the peer edit.

(LESSON EXTENSION)

✛ Celebrate students' memoirs with a Walk Down Memory Lane bulletin board. Hang their memoirs on a quaint, meandering road made from butcher paper. Suggest that students illustrate their memoirs with photos of the setting or original drawings.

Simile

> A **simile** is a comparison of two dissimilar things using the words *like* or *as*.

"'Ravi beta, you are as warm as a newborn kid, as soft as the frangipani blossom, as sweet as the juice of the mango.'"

from *Elephant Dance: Memories of India* by Theresa Heine

Selected Literature

Elephant Dance: Memories of India by Theresa Heine, illustrated by Sheila Moxley, 2004, Barefoot Books

Curious Ravi floods his grandfather with questions about India. As his grandfather lovingly answers each one, Ravi and the reader journey through this magical land, vicariously experiencing the richness of its geography and culture.

Other Possible Literature Selections

Across the Alley by Richard Michelson, illustrated by E. B. Lewis, 2006, G. P. Putnam's Sons

Two boys—Willie, who is African American, and Abe, who is Jewish—secretly play together at night, teaching each other how to pitch a baseball and how to play the violin. When Abe's grandfather discovers the boys' friendship, he soon realizes that Abe is a great pitcher, and Willie is the true master of the violin.

Grizz! by Eric A. Kimmel, illustrated by Andrew Glass, 2000, Holiday House

In this hilarious retelling of a traditional folktale, Lucky Doolin makes a bargain with a stranger. For seven years he does not shave, shower, or trim his nails so he can accumulate enough money to marry his sweetheart.

Lesson Idea

To introduce simile, write several examples on the board or give each student an index card containing one as they enter the classroom. Consider using the following examples:

> The snow fell from the sky like a parade of tiny, silky parachutes.

> In the sunlight, the lines on Grandpa's forehead looked as deep as the crisp creases in my dad's khaki pants.

> The wind whistled like a speeding train racing toward its final destination.

> Grandma's hugs were as warm as an enormous downy quilt on a blustery day.

First, define the term, and then model how to interpret similes: *When I read a simile, first I think about which two objects are being compared. In the simile "The snow fell from the sky like a parade of tiny, silky parachutes" snowflakes are being compared to tiny parachutes. Then I think about how those two objects are alike. Snowflakes and parachutes are really light, so that's one similarity. Also, since the simile refers to a "parade" of parachutes, I know that the sky is filled with snowflakes. Another similarity is that snowflakes float down to earth, and parachutes do, too. This simile helps me visualize tiny, soft snowflakes sweeping across the sky.*

After modeling, discuss each simile in detail. Ask students to identify the simile, state which two things are being compared, and explain the similarities between them. Encourage students to describe or draw the image the simile conveys.

Before, During, and After Reading

Before you read *Elephant Dance: Memories of India* aloud, give a brief overview of the story. Explain that through Ravi's questions about India and his grandfather's answers, the reader learns about this enchanting country. Explain that the story is full of rich similes, some of which are unique to the Indian culture. As students listen to the story, have them write down the similes they hear.

After reading, make a list of the similes students offer on chart paper or the board. If the list is incomplete, go back to the story and add to it. Here are some examples of similes from the book:

MATERIALS

❐ Simile Planning Sheet, p.14 (optional)

❐ white cardstock

REPRODUCIBLES

Students

❐ Students: Postcard Template, p. 69

Teaching Literary Elements With Picture Books

"At dawn [the sun] rolls into the sky like a fiery ball." (page 1)

"Like a wild horse, [the wind] stamps and snorts." (page 7)

"The monsoon rain is like a curtain, silver like Anjali's bangles." (page 9)

"[The monsoon rain] cascades like a waterfall from the sky, making mirrors of the ground." (page 9)

"I am old, brown like garden soil, and wrinkled as a walnut." (pages 19–20)

"'Ravi beta, you are as warm as a newborn kid, as soft as the frangipani blossom, as sweet as the juice of a mango.'" (page 27)

Assign small groups of students a simile from the list to interpret and draw. To assist students with this process, post the guidelines at right for interpreting similes.

Before some groups

Guidelines for Interpreting Similes
1. Identify the simile.
2. Decide which two things are being compared.
3. Discuss the similarities between the two things.
4. Draw what the simile makes you see.

discuss their assigned simile, they may have to do some quick research. If a computer is available, the "monsoon" and "frangipani" groups can find information about their topics at the following Wikipedia Web pages:

http://en.wikipedia.org/wiki/Monsoon

http://en.wikipedia.org/wiki/Frangipani

If classroom computers are not available, have other resources (i.e., dictionary, nonfiction books, magazines, newspapers, and so on) that students can use to research the information they'll need to understand the simile.

Encourage each student within a group to draw the assigned simile; this will help illustrate that readers can interpret similes in different ways.

Writing Activity

Invite students to create simile postcards. Ideally, the content of the postcard should relate to a country or place students have been studying in social studies. Students may also research a country of interest or write about a place they have visited and know well.

Once students choose the place and the person to whom they will write, model writing a postcard similar to the one on page 14, which uses information from *Elephant Dance: Memories of India* as the basis for the content.

June 9, 2007

Dear Mom and Dad,

Greetings from New Delhi! As I write, I am devouring a saffron-colored mango that tastes as rich and sweet as 100% pure Vermont maple syrup. This morning we visited the famous Lotus Temple, a stunning replica of the Indian national flower. From the front, the petals look like light rays from a falling star.

Today the city is experiencing one of its famous heat waves. Consequently, I am as red as a fire hydrant and just as hot. When I go back to the hotel, I think I'll hail a taxi or ride one of the popular auto rickshaws, a simple canvas-topped golf cart.

Well, here comes our tour guide, so I have to sign off now. Our next destination is Humayun's Tomb. Everyone says it resembles the Taj Mahal. I can't wait to see it!

Miss you both!

Love,

John

The Rodriguez Family

12830 Sagebrush Trail

Fort Sage, Oklahoma   73456

Ask students to identify the similes in your postcard. Discuss the importance of using original similes in writing, not tired, overused ones, such as "red as a rose" or "bright as the sun."

To help students construct original similes for their postcards, consider creating a Simile Planning Sheet like the one below:

Simile Planning Sheet

1. _____ is like _____ .
   (name of country or place)

2. The weather is as _____ as _____ .

3. The _____ taste(s) as _____ as _____ .
   (specific food)

4. The _____ is as _____ as _____ .
   (landform)

5. My favorite _____ is like _____ .
   (tourist attraction/favorite site)

Before beginning the drafting process, pair students and have them evaluate the similes on their planning sheets. Introduce the following questions to guide the peer feedback:

Are the similes original?

What two things are being compared?

What similarities do the two things have?

Does the comparison make sense?

As they draft, remind students that they should use two or three similes— but they are not required to force similes from the prewriting practice into their postcard; the similes should fit naturally into the piece. After drafting and revising, students can publish and colorfully illustrate their postcards on white cardstock copies of the Postcard Template. Display the final postcards on a large world map.

(LESSON EXTENSIONS)

✚ To connect *Elephant Dance: Memories of India* to the social studies curriculum, have students research a country of interest or a country they are studying. Ask them to gather information about the geography, culture, religion, animals and plants, and food. If you desire, form jigsaw groups to do the research, and have each member of the group focus on a single topic related to the country, such as geography, to become the group expert. After students have completed their research, they can create fact-and-sketch booklets modeled after the "Living in India" section (pages 33–37) of *Elephant Dance: Memories of India*. Use the booklets as a classroom reference resource.

✚ Another idea is to have students create Simile Travel Brochures.

Metaphor

> A **metaphor** is a comparison of two dissimilar objects that does not use the words *like* or *as*.

"The ocean is . . . A GARDEN . . ."

from *The Ocean Is . . .* by Kathleen W. Kranking

✳ ✳ ✳

Selected Literature

The Ocean Is . . . by Kathleen W. Kranking, photographs by Norbert Wu, 2003, Henry Holt

The author uses a variety of metaphors to describe the characteristics of the ocean. Metaphors such as "the ocean is a playground" and "the ocean is a galaxy" are enhanced by exquisite photographs of the ocean.

Other Possible Literature Selections

Prairie Train by Marsha Wilson Chall, illustrated by John Thompson, 2003, HarperCollins

While riding the Great Northern from her country home to her grandmother's house in the city, a young girl paints a stunning, detailed picture of the elegant train and spectacular landscape.

In November by Cynthia Rylant, illustrated by Jill Kastner, 2000, Harcourt

In November the earth begins to make its winter bed to protect and nurture its children. Through poetic text rich with imagery, Rylant celebrates the quiet beauty of November and the love inspired through family gatherings and celebrations.

Lesson Idea

To acquaint students with the concept of metaphor, post the following examples on the board or chart paper, or create your own:

The cafeteria is an exploding firecracker.

Homework is a pile of dirty laundry.

The gym is a herd of stampeding elephants.

The music room is a set of screeching tires.

The hallway is a can of sardines.

Ask students what they observe about all of these sentences. Guide them to discover that one thing is being compared to something dissimilar in each sentence. Discuss several of these metaphors, focusing on what is being compared and which features each item has that make them comparable.

MATERIALS

❏ "Metaphor" by Eve Merriam (in *Wonderful Words: Poems about Reading, Writing, Speaking, and Listening* selected by Lee Bennett Hopkins and illustrated by Karen Barbour, 2004, Simon & Schuster Books for Young Readers)

❏ Metaphor Planning Sheet, p. 18 (optional)

❏ Peer Editing Form, p. 19

REPRODUCIBLES

Students

❏ Understanding Metaphors, p. 70

Before, During, and After Reading

It can be difficult for students to construct extended metaphors. Before writing original metaphors, they need practice identifying and interpreting metaphors to understand what they are and how they operate. Therefore, prior to reading *The Ocean Is . . .* aloud, distribute a copy of the Understanding Metaphors graphic organizer to each student. Explain that in the book you're going to read to them the author uses ten metaphors to describe the ocean. Read pages 4–10 out loud and

Name _____ Date _____

Understanding Metaphors

Metaphor	What two things are being compared?	How are they alike?	What idea is the author trying to convey?
The ocean is a playground.	the ocean and a playground	People play games on a playground, and animals play games in the ocean. Recess occurs on the playground and in the ocean.	In the ocean, animals have fun just like people do on land.

70

then stop. Use an overhead projector or a document camera to display the metaphor on page 6 if multiple copies of the book are not available. With the class, complete the first section of the graphic organizer as depicted on page 17.

Follow the same procedure to analyze the metaphor on page 8. Then have pairs complete the graphic organizer for the metaphors on pages 12 and 14. Allow time for pairs to share their responses with the rest of the class.

Writing Activity

Using the text structure in *The Ocean Is . . .* as a scaffold, have students create three metaphors on a content-related topic such as space, the rainforest, quadrilaterals, parts of speech, or a musical concept. A model appears below.

An adjective is . . . A PAINTBRUSH

Splashing rich, vibrant color

Across a sea of lifeless nouns

Creating stunning landscapes and portraits

That transcend time and endure forever.

For struggling writers or younger students, use well-known objects, such as a pencil sharpener, sunflower, sponge, or chair to create original metaphors. Create one metaphor with the whole class first before having students work independently or with a partner. To help all students construct metaphors, consider providing them with a simple Metaphor Planning Sheet similar to the one shown below.

```
┌─────────────────────────────────────────────────────────┐
│              Metaphor Planning Sheet                      │
│                                                           │
│   The _____ is . . . A _____        │
│                                                           │
│   _____     │
│                                                           │
│   _____     │
│                                                           │
│   _____     │
│                                                           │
│   _____     │
└─────────────────────────────────────────────────────────┘
```

After students draft their metaphors, have pairs or groups use a peer editing form like the model on the next page to evaluate the effectiveness of their metaphors.

Peer Editing Form

Writer's Name _____ Editor's Name _____

1. Which two things are being compared?

   _____

2. How effective is the metaphor? Does it make sense?

   _____

3. What idea is the writer trying to convey?

   _____

4. What changes or revisions would you recommend?

   _____

Provide time for students to revise and polish their pieces based on the peer editing.

One way to publish students' completed metaphors is to create a Metaphor Mural. Roll out a large mural-size sheet of butcher paper and assign a space for each student to write and illustrate his or her metaphor. To illustrate the metaphors, students may use paint, magazine photos, newspaper clippings, and original photos and artwork. If students download images from the Internet, remind them to abide by all copyright laws. Encourage students to be creative in their designs. Some may want to incorporate the metaphor into the illustration. Display the completed mural in the hallway or in the school library.

(LESSON EXTENSIONS)

✤ At the beginning of the school year, create a Myself in Metaphors mural. Have students use metaphors to describe themselves and then illustrate these metaphors with pictures or photos representing various stages of their lives.

✤ Read Eve Merriam's poem "Metaphor." Encourage students to imitate Merriam's structure and create a poem about another time of day.

Personification

Personification is a figure of speech in which nonhuman objects are given human qualities.

"New York put his feet up and smiled at the evening."

from *New York Is English, Chattanooga Is Creek* by Chris Raschka

✳ ✳ ✳

Selected Literature

New York Is English, Chattanooga Is Creek written and illustrated by Chris Raschka, 2005, Atheneum

Tea-drinking New York hosts a party and invites cities from all over the United States to attend including Princess Charlotte, Pushy Saint Louis, and Motherly Miami.

Other Possible Literature Selections

Cave by Diane Siebert, illustrated by Wayne McLoughlin, 2000, HarperCollins

In stunning poetic language, the author personifies the life, feelings, and physical features of a cave. The description of the cave's inhabitants and the splendor of its inner beauty are enhanced by breath-taking acrylic paintings.

Hello, Harvest Moon by Ralph Fletcher, illustrated by Kate Kiesler, 2003, Clarion Books

"With silent slippers" the full moon "climbs the night stairs," casting a magical glow across the land. Consequently, the reader sees the nighttime landscape and people from the moon's perspective.

Lesson Idea

. . . .

To introduce the concept of personification, have students do quick sketches of well-known examples of personification, such as the following:

REPRODUCIBLES

Students and Teacher
- ❏ City Research Organizer, p. 71
- ❏ City Character Profile, p. 72

the sun smiles down on me

tree branches dance in the breeze

the ocean's arms embrace the beachgoers

Next, ask students to share their sketches with a partner and identify the human qualities the object has. Then define personification, emphasizing the fact that the word *person* is contained within the term. Associate the word *person* with the human qualities students identified in the examples to solidify the definition.

Before, During, and After Reading

Before you introduce *New York Is English, Chattanooga Is Creek* to the class, write several of the cities' names and origins from the Guest List on pages 3 and 4 of the book on chart paper and post them in various places around the room. As students enter the classroom, invite them to read the names and origins, explain they are part of a guest list in a book, and ask the class to predict what the book will be about.

Ask students to listen closely as you read the story and jot down the human characteristics that New York possesses to help them deepen their understanding of personification. On page 11, stop reading and ask students to share their lists. Continue reading to discover more of New York's character traits.

After reading, discuss examples of personification as they relate to some of the other cities described in the story. List these examples on the board. Emphasize that through personification, these cities actually possess their own unique personality traits and so it seems plausible that they could be guests at a party.

Writing Activity

Have each student choose a city to research. Since research involves searching for answers to questions, tell students to look through different resources to discover the answers to the questions on the City Research Organizer. After the research is completed and students know their city well, have them personify the city and bring it to life by completing a City Character Profile reproducible.

After students have completed the City Character Profile, invite them to write a story about their character that includes information about the city. As students engage in the writing process, be certain that they peer conference and share suggestions as needed. Share student writing in a class book, or post the work on a bulletin board.

(LESSON EXTENSIONS)

✚ Host a City Celebration by asking students to become their city character. On the day of the party, they can dress up as their character and take on its persona. Simple costumes might include a sash or T-shirt with the city's name written on it and decorated with pictures of the city and/or objects related to it. Party conversation should be geared toward conveying information about students' cities. To guide the conversations, students can refer to their character profiles. Commemorate the event by appointing class photographers to take pictures. Use the photos to create a Personification album.

✚ Have students create a travel brochure that employs personification. They can include a map of the destination as well as the location's famous sights, people, food, and events. When describing the landforms and physical features, encourage students to use first-person narration and imitate Diane Siebert's style in *Cave*.

Irony

Irony is defined as the opposite of what is expected. In verbal irony, words mean the opposite of what is intended. In situational irony, an event is the opposite of what is expected. In dramatic irony, the reader (or audience) knows more about what is happening than the characters do.

A classic example of dramatic irony can be found in *Romeo and Juliet*. The audience is aware that Juliet drank a sleeping potion and is not dead. However, Romeo thinks she is dead. This knowledge makes Romeo's death all the more heartbreaking.

✳ ✳ ✳

Selected Literature

Pig Tale written and illustrated by Helen Oxenbury, 2005, Margaret K. McElderry Books

Two poor and bored pigs discover a treasure and are catapulted into a life of luxury. Ironically, they discover they prefer their simple life and go from riches to rags.

Other Possible Literature Selections

Whatever written and illustrated by William Bee, 2005, Candlewick Press

Difficult-to-please Billy responds with "Whatever" even when he flies to the end of outer space. However, when he encounters the world's hungriest tiger and says, "Whatever," Billy meets his match and is swallowed whole.

School Lunch written and illustrated by True Kelley, 2005, Holiday House

Tired of trying to serve complaining students, Harriet the cook goes on vacation. Substitute cooks prepare such feasts as lumpy creamed spinach and fish heads, causing the students to beg Harriet to come back and prepare their food. When Harriet returns, students happily devour healthy lunches.

Lesson Idea

To acquaint students with the difficult concept of irony, prepare a set of index cards that contain examples of ironic situations, such as the ones listed below:

Two people on a desert island are surrounded by water yet are dying of thirst.

A young couple wins the lottery but later goes bankrupt.

Sixteen-year-old twins receive a pair of brand-new BMW convertibles for their birthday but then fail their driving tests.

MATERIALS
Optional:
❏ costumes
❏ material for sets and sound effects
❏ video camera
❏ material for awards

REPRODUCIBLES
Students
❏ Instantly Ironic organizer, p. 73

When a family arrives at the ice cream store on the hottest day of the year, the air conditioner breaks and the last scoop of ice cream is sold before the family is served.

Then distribute one card to each pair of students and take one yourself. Model acting out the ironic situation on your card. Provide two to three minutes for partners to decide how they will act out their scenario for the class. After each presentation, ask students what the character(s) in each scenario intended or expected to happen and what actually happened. Lead students toward discovering that in each situation, the opposite of what was expected occurred. Use this activity as an introduction to the concept of irony. (Since the selected literature depicts situational irony and since students will use situational irony in the writing activity, focus on this definition.) After defining the term, have students give various examples of irony from movies, television shows, and books.

Before, During, and After Reading

Before reading *Pig Tale* out loud, ask students to listen for examples of irony in the story and to identify the overall irony of the situation. Ask them to pay attention to how the author structures the tale, particularly noting the climax and full-circle ending.

During reading, stop on page 10 after the line, "You will find it simpler than jewels when you pay." Ask students to identify the irony of this situation. Continue reading until the pigs are in bed and Briggs cannot sleep because of the heat. Stop again, asking students to explain the irony in this situation.

After completing the story, lead the class in a discussion in which students identify the climax of the story and note the author's techniques for creating the turning point. Ask students to identify other examples of irony they noticed and to point out the overall irony of the situation in the tale.

Writing Activity

Ask students to imagine that they are a playwright or a screenwriter. Tell them that they are going to create a short one- or two-page script that shows situational irony. Pair students and ask each pair to think of a situation in which the opposite of what is expected or intended happens. For example, a criminal falls in love with the police chief's daughter; a young man marries a woman he thought was a complete nerd in high school; or a volunteer firefighter's house burns down while she is out fighting a fire.

As soon as the pairs come up with an example of situational irony, ask them to share it with a different pair. Have these peer evaluators review the example to be sure the outcome is the opposite of what is expected. To differentiate instruction for students struggling to come up with an original example, allow these pairs to use one of the scenarios listed in the Lesson Idea section or one of the examples generated during the discussion of *Pig Tale*.

After pairs check each other's examples, help them begin the process of thinking like a playwright or a screenwriter by modeling how to complete the Instantly Ironic graphic organizer.

Using the graphic organizer as a foundation, have partners compose a script, revise it, type a final version, and print two copies. After an adequate amount of practice time, have the partners perform a dramatic reading of the script in front of the class. At the conclusion of each performance, challenge the class to identify the situational irony.

(LESSON EXTENSIONS)

✚ Have partners create simple costumes, set designs, and sound effects, and then practice their play or screen performances until they are camera ready. Then videotape the performances.

✚ Following all regulations regarding students' privacy rights to ensure their protection, upload the videotape onto a teacher or school Web page for parents or guardians to view.

✚ Ask student film critics to write reviews of the performances and publish them. To celebrate student successes, have a night at the Oscars and Tonys and present awards for the most original screenplay or play, best actor and actress, most creative sound effects, best set design, and so on.

Theme

> **Theme** is the author's message to the reader; it's a statement about life or humanity.

An example of theme in *The School Is Not White! A True Story of the Civil Rights Movement* by Doreen Rappaport is that courage and determination can defeat injustice.

✳ ✳ ✳

Selected Literature

The School Is Not White! A True Story of the Civil Rights Movement by Doreen Rappaport, illustrated by Curtis James, 2005, Hyperion

In segregated Drew, Mississippi, Matthew and Mae Bertha Carter decide to send their seven school-age children to an all-white school. Battling prejudice, injustice, and loneliness, the parents courageously pursue the goal of attaining a quality education for their children.

Other Possible Literature Selections

Rosa by Nikki Giovanni, illustrated by Bryan Collier, 2005, Henry Holt

Stitched into the fabric of Rosa Parks's story, the history of the Civil Rights movement unfolds in this beautifully written and illustrated biography.

This Is the Dream by Diane Z. Shore and Jessica Alexander, illustrated by James Ransome, 2006, HarperCollins

Through stunning paintings and collages and a lyric text that spans the years of segregation and Jim Crow Laws to the present time, the authors and illustrator convey the powerful results of nonviolent change.

Lesson Idea

· · · · · · · · · · · · · ·

As students enter the room, give them a slip of
paper with a theme written on it, such as "Treat
others the way you want to be treated"; "Money
cannot buy happiness"; or "Good judgment
comes from experience, but experience comes
from poor judgment." Form small groups, and
have members share these statements with each
other. Ask what the statements have in common.
Guide the groups to discover that these are
general statements about life, or themes. As a
class, define the term *theme*.

MATERIALS
❏ colored masking tape
❏ print or video copy of Dr. Martin Luther King Jr.'s, "I Have a Dream" speech

REPRODUCIBLES
Students
❏ Writing With a Theme, p. 74

Before, During, and After Reading

To activate students' prior knowledge and to help them make personal connections
to *The School Is Not White!*, ask them to write a journal entry about a time in their
lives when they wanted to give up on something. If necessary, provide some
examples of situations to prompt students before writing. After students share their
entries with a partner, ask for volunteers to do a whole-class share. They will
expand on these entries in the Writing Activity.

Introduce *The School Is Not White!,* explaining that the children in the book want
to give up on something. Show the cover of the book, read the title, and ask
students to predict what they think the author's message will be. List their
responses on chart paper or on the board.

Tell students that as you read, they are to listen for examples of life lessons that
the author conveys. They should also reflect upon their previous predictions and
consider any revisions they want to make, based on the content of the story.

After reading, provide small groups of students with chart paper and markers
and have them construct a theme web. In the center of the web, the group will
write a theme from the text. Then ask students to find at least four details from the
story to support the theme and write these in the web. Hang the webs around the
room, and send students on a gallery tour of them. As a whole class, discuss the
themes of the text.

Teaching Literary Elements With Picture Books

Writing Activity

Using the journal entries they wrote before the read-aloud as a starting point, students can write personal narratives about an obstacle they have faced and describe how they felt when they tried to overcome it. To guide students in the process, distribute the graphic organizer Writing With a Theme. Use *The School Is Not White!* to model how to use the organizer before students proceed.

After students draft, revise, and edit their narratives, consider publishing the pieces in a class book modeled after the Chicken Soup for the Soul series. Sponsor a book cover contest.

(LESSON EXTENSIONS)

✚ Have students compose theme songs or raps that convey the message in the selected text. Think about using the song "We Shall Overcome" as a model for this activity.

✚ Challenge students to write fables designed to teach a life lesson, but tell them not to attach a moral to it. Read the fables out loud in class or in small groups and have the audience suggest a moral for it.

✚ Construct a theme quilt. Cut a class set of 5-inch squares. Have each student write a theme from the selected literature on the bottom of a square and illustrate it. Glue the squares onto a large sheet of rectangular butcher paper. Use colored masking tape to make a border. A variation on this activity is to read an illustrated version of Dr. Martin Luther King, Jr.'s, "I Have a Dream" speech or to show a video of it and create a quilt based on the themes present in the speech.

Idiom

An **idiom** is an expression whose meaning it not literal.

"Eloise had a craving for snails, but she accidentally opened a can of worms."

from *Monkey Business* written and illustrated by Wallace Edwards

Selected Literature

Monkey Business written and illustrated by Wallace Edwards, 2004, Kids Can Press

With its visual feast of twenty-four idioms and detailed glossary, this book is sure to delight even the reluctant reader.

Other Possible Literature Selections

Even More Parts written and illustrated by Tedd Arnold, 2004, Dial Books

This humorous story portrays a young boy's fears of idioms. When he hears idiomatic expressions such as "my stomach is growling" and "I sang my heart out," he interprets them literally and shares his hilarious imaginings with the reader.

There's a Frog in My Throat: 440 Animal Sayings a Little Bird Told Me written by Loreen Leedy and Pat Street, illustrated by Loreen Leedy, 2003, Holiday House

An entertaining collection of similes, metaphors, idioms, and proverbs is coupled with whimsical illustrations in this fun-filled text.

Lesson Idea

Activate background knowledge of idioms by repeating an idiomatic expression such as "It's raining cats and dogs." Have students draw a quick sketch to show what this expression literally and figuratively means (see the examples below). If necessary, review the concepts of literal and figurative interpretations. In the idiom, *James turned green with envy*, the literal interpretation would be that James's skin actually turned green; the figurative interpretation would be that James desperately wanted something that somebody else had.

Literal interpretation	Figurative interpretation

Invite students to share their sketches with partners, and then ask them to imagine how they would feel if they were from another country and heard this expression. Explain that many countries have similar figures of speech that pertain to their own unique cultures. For example, in Ireland, the phrase *He's only winding you* means "He's trying to irritate or anger you." Another example comes from Chile, where the phrase *Milk from the foot of the cow* means that the milk is extremely fresh. Visit the following Web site for additional phrases and interpretations: http://www.eslcafe.com.

Encourage students to share any idioms they know. On chart paper, record class-generated examples of idioms in a two-column chart that shows the literal and figurative interpretation of each idiom. If you need to jump start the discussion, write the following idioms on the chart:

I hit the wall.   It cost an arm and a leg.   Toe the line.

Lead the class in a discussion about the "silly" phrase (literal meaning) and then talk about what the phrase figuratively means. For example, to demonstrate the literal meaning of *I hit the wall*, have a student walk up to a wall in the classroom and pretend to bump into it. Then discuss the idiom's figurative meaning, explaining if necessary that people use this expression when they run into a situation or a problem and cannot make any more progress.

Before, During, and After Reading

Prior to reading *Monkey Business*, inform students that they will need to pay close attention to how the author/illustrator visually interprets the literal meaning of each idiom. Also remind them to listen for the idiomatic phrases presented in the book. Ask students to ponder why Wallace Edwards might have titled the book *Monkey Business*.

As you read, discuss the relationship between some of the illustrations and the idioms (but be sure to save some for groups to interpret later). For example, on page 8 the illustration shows a dog playing the violin with his ears. The text reads: "Phil had no formal musical training, so he learned to play by ear."

Assign small groups of students one or two of the idioms from the text to interpret. Invite groups to write their interpretations on an overhead transparency to share with the class. After sharing, distribute the "meanings" section from the glossary in *Monkey Business*, and let students compare these with their own interpretations.

Writing Activity

Follow the steps below to create a *Class Book of Idioms*:

1. Allow each student to select a different idiom to illustrate both figuratively and literally. Be sure to avoid duplications. Use resources such as *The Scholastic Dictionary of Idioms* by Marvin Terban to assist students with their selections.

2. Explain that students are to create one page of a book designed to help younger students explore idioms. Each page will contain the following three items:

   ◆ An illustration of the literal meaning

   ◆ An illustration of the figurative meaning

   ◆ The idiom itself used in the context of a sentence

Literal illustration
Figurative illustration
IDIOM: After school, students sat in the bleachers and CHEWED THE FAT.

3. After students submit a quick sketch or draft of their ideas for the page, provide feedback before they work on the final version.

4. Bind and present the final product to a classroom of younger students. Celebrate by having each student read his or her page to the younger class.

(LESSON EXTENSIONS)

✚ Encourage students to identify the monkeys that appear on each page of *Monkey Business* to see how they connect to the meaning and title of the book.

✚ Hold a class Idiom Day. As students walk in the door, hand them a slip of paper with an idiom written on it. Have pairs of students explain their idioms to one another. For the remainder of the class, reward students with a bonus point each time they use an idiom. At the end of class, reward the person with the most points with a small prize.

✚ Bookmark the following Web site for students to visit at the computer center: http://www.funbrain.com/idioms/index.html.

✚ Invite students to play Idiom Charades. Prepare sets of cards with idiomatic expressions written on them for teams of students to act out (some suggestions appear below). Explain that the class will play charades to see how many idiomatic expressions they know. Review the procedure for playing the game of Charades, if necessary. Each team member will draw a card with an idiomatic phrase and act out its literal meaning for the team to guess— without talking. Give teams a time limit of one minute to correctly guess the idiom. Here is a list of popular idioms that can be used for Idiom Charades.

pull my leg	shake a leg	don't get bent out of shape
be all thumbs	let off the hook	get off on the wrong foot
be all ears	be on the ball	let the cat out of the bag
be on thin ice	drag your feet	drive me up the wall
hold your horses	get off my back	butterflies in my stomach
a heart of gold	under the weather	get up on the wrong side of the bed
back-seat driver	frog in my throat	open a can of worms
paint the town red	have a green thumb	cat got your tongue

don't count your chickens before they hatch

Hyperbole

Hyperbole is a deliberate exaggeration used to emphasize a point or to create an effect.

"[The infant] Rose snored up plenty that first night breathing on her own, rattling the rafters on the roof along with the booming thunder."

from *Thunder Rose* by Jerdine Nolen

✳ ✳ ✳

Selected Literature

Thunder Rose by Jerdine Nolen, illustrated by Kadir Nelson, 2003, Harcourt

The world's strongest little girl discovers how to use her "song of thunder" to overcome and calm a terrible storm.

Other Literature Selections

Lies and Other Tall Tales, written and illustrated by Christopher Myers, 2005, HarperCollins

Myers's stunning collages accurately portray the hyperbole in this unusual collection of tall tales that he's adapted. The tales were originally collected by Zora Neale Hurston during her travels through the Gulf States in the 1930s.

Dona Flor by Pat Mora, illustrated by Raúl Colón, 2005, Knopf

Meet Dona Flor, a giant woman who is one of the kindest and most generous people in her village. But when an intruder enters, she is the one to restore order.

Lesson Idea

. . . .

MATERIALS

❏ Graphic Organizer for Tall Tales, p. 36

Activate students' background knowledge of the hyperbole used in tall tales and folk tales by writing the following phrase on the board:

HE WAS SO BIG THAT _____.

Challenge pairs of students to discuss how to make this person really seem *bigger* than life. As a whole class, share ideas of how to complete the sentence.

Then have partners complete the following two statements in their writing notebook or on loose leaf paper:

SHE WAS SO SMALL THAT _____.

THE STUDENT WAS SO LOUD THAT _____.

Invite pairs to turn to another pair to share their ideas. Then ask these groups of four to choose one statement to share with the entire class and to write it on a sticky note. Appoint one group member to orally share the statement with the rest of the class. Have this individual post the group's sticky note on a piece of chart paper so the class can refer to it during the writing activity.

As a class, discuss what the statements have in common. Steer students toward the idea of *exaggeration*. Explain that they have created statements called hyperboles and then share the definition. Emphasize that hyperbole is the foundation of tall tales and is often used in humorous writing as well.

Before, During, and After Reading

After the above warm-up activity, read pages 8–14 in *Lies and Other Tall Tales*, beginning with the section "What's the biggest man you've ever seen?" and ending with "He was so mean, he greased another man and swallowed him whole." Conduct a whole-class discussion comparing these descriptions to the ones developed earlier by students.

Transition into a read-aloud of *Thunder Rose*. Before reading, distribute an index card to each student. Write the word *hyperbole* on the board, and have students write it in large letters on their index cards. Tell them to listen for examples of hyperbole during the read-aloud and to hold up their index card when they hear one. After the read-aloud, discuss the hyperboles in the book. Once students provide several examples of hyperbole, begin the writing activity.

Writing Activity

Tell students they are going to write an original tall tale that uses hyperbole. To begin this process, use *Thunder Rose* to help students identify the characteristics of a tall tale. Begin by asking them what makes a tall tale like *Thunder Rose* different from other stories. Elicit responses similar to the following: the main character, Rose, has superhuman powers and performs impossible tasks; the author uses exaggeration and humor; many of the events are unbelievable and couldn't happen in real life. List student-generated characteristics on the board or a sheet of chart paper. Use the characteristics to construct a graphic organizer similar to the one shown at right.

Use *Thunder Rose* to model how to complete the graphic organizer before students tackle it on their own. Then have them follow the steps in the writing process to develop individual tall tales. Tall tales can also be written in pairs or in small groups.

Graphic Organizer for Tall Tales

Main Character: _____

Description: _____

Exaggerated Traits and Abilities:

_____

_____

_____

Other Characteristics:

_____

_____

_____

Setting: _____

Place: _____ Time: _____

Plot: _____

_____

Events:

1. _____

2. _____

3. _____

4. _____

Resolution: _____

_____

Sample Graphic Organizer for Tall Tales

(LESSON EXTENSIONS)

✚ Celebrate by sharing students' tall tales with a younger audience or with parents/guardians. For younger children, develop Tall Tale Totes to send home that include a comment book and a taped recording of each child reading his or her tale and a copy of the tale. Encourage older students to read their tall tale to a younger sibling or neighbor for extra credit. On a sheet of paper, have the listener rate the tale on a scale of 1–5 with 5 being the highest. Also tell readers to ask listeners to provide a reason for the rating and to initial the paper.

Onomatopoeia

> **Onomatopoeia** refers to a word that imitates the sound of the object or the action it names.

"'Clackety clack clack clack.' Yes, I'm riding the rails!"

from *Langston's Train Ride* by Robert Burleigh

✳ ✳ ✳

Selected Literature

Langston's Train Ride by Robert Burleigh, illustrated by Leonard Jenkins, 2004, Orchard Books

Sounds of the train fuel Langston Hughes's imagination and inspire him to write his first poem.

Other Possible Literature Selections:

Arctic Lights, Arctic Nights by Debbie S. Miller, illustrated by Jon Van Zyle, 2003, Walker & Company

Transporting the reader on a yearlong journey through the Arctic, this nonfiction text exquisitely portrays the landscape and animals of the region, using onomatopoeia to begin a description of each Arctic animal.

Snow Sounds: An Onomatopoeic Story written and illustrated by David A. Johnson, 2006, Houghton Mifflin

Breaking the silence associated with a fresh snow fall, snow removal machines rev their engines to make way for the school bus. Onomatopoeic words splash across this book's stunning water colors as the machines plow, scrape, and blow.

Lesson Idea

Explain that *Langston's Train Ride* shows how the sounds of the train inspired Langston Hughes, a Harlem Renaissance poet, to write his first poem "The Negro Speaks of Rivers." You can duplicate a copy of the poem or listen to it here: http://www. poets.org/viewmedia.php/prmMID/15722. Share the poem with the class and then discuss it.

MATERIALS

❑ audio or print copy of "The Negro Speaks of Rivers" by Langston Hughes

❑ transparency of Guidelines for Creating Found Poetry, p. 38

Before, During, and After Reading

Before reading *Langston's Train Ride* aloud, ask students what kind of sounds trains make and create a list of these sounds. Blow a train whistle or download and play train sounds from the Internet to stimulate the discussion. Once the list is compiled, define the term *onomatopoeia* and share other examples, such as *meow, crash, sizzle, crunch, boom,* and *buzz.*

Ask students to make a list of the examples of onomatopoeia they hear as they listen to the book *Langston's Train Ride.* If possible, have multiple copies of the text available, or use a document camera to project the book onto a screen as you read. After reading, have students share their lists with the rest of the class.

Writing Activity

Revisit *Langston's Train Ride* and, following the guidelines below, create a class "found poem" comprised of phrases taken directly from the text that contain examples of onomatopoeia.

Guidelines for Creating Found Poetry
1. Make a list of onomatopoeic words and phrases from the text.
2. Place them on a page line by line in the form of a poem.
3. Read the poem aloud.
4. Decide if and how you want to revise your poem. For example, you might want to rearrange the lines, substitute more powerful verbs, or add repetition for effect.

Here's an example of a found poem based on *Langston's Train Ride* to help guide your instruction. All the lines are taken directly from the text and include examples of onomatopoeia.

Train Ride

Clackety clack clack
Clickety clickety clack
Riding the rails.
Whooo! Whooo!
The train **rumbles, rumbles, rumbles**
West, west, west,
Bumping and swaying
Twisting and turning
Roaring like an angry dragon
Slowing now
Clackety clack clack
Clickety click click
A soothing, rhythmic sound.
As the wheels **hum**,
My eyelids slowly close
Like ancient shades.
Plush, velvety cushions cradle me
As I drift back, back
And back some more
Into sweet oblivion
Completely at peace
In my womblike sanctuary.

(a found poem based on *Langston's Train Ride* written by
Robert Burleigh and illustrated by Leonard Jenkins

After the class creates an onomatopoeic found poem, students can do a choral reading of it using musical instruments or objects to imitate the sounds.

Additional references for found poetry appear below:

Dunning, S., & Stafford, W. (1992). *Getting the knack: 20 poetry writing exercises.* Urbana, IL: National Council of Teachers of English

Yopp, H., & Yopp, R.H. (2006). *Literature-based reading activities (4th Ed.).* Boston: Pearson, Allyn, & Bacon

AU / LCCC
Teacher Educational Resource Center
1005 North Abbe Road
LR 216
Elyria, Ohio 44035
440-366-4082

Onomatopoeia   **39**

(LESSON EXTENSION)

✛ Have students write individual poems that use onomatopoeia. Celebrate their poetry by hosting an Onomatopoeic Poetry Party. Create an invitation for the performance that contains onomatopoeia. Have students read and perform their poems using sound effects and musical instruments to highlight the onomatopoeic sounds.

✛ Challenge pairs or small groups to write narrative text to accompany the pictures and sounds in *Snow Sounds: An Onomatopoeic Story*. Remind them to include the onomatopoeic word from the story in their narratives and encourage them to add more.

✛ If using *Langston's Train Ride* as part of a unit on the Harlem Renaissance, immerse the class in the music and art of that historic period. Create a PowerPoint display, bring in art books and posters, or have students research artists, photographers, and sculptors such as Aaron Douglas, Palmer Hayden, William Johnson, Lois Mailou Jones, Jacob Lawrence, Archibald Motley, James Van Der Zee, and Augusta Savage. Play jazz by Louis Armstrong, Billie Holiday, Josephine Baker, Duke Ellington, Dizzie Gillespie, and Charlie Parker. Extensive links to Web sites and lesson ideas related to the Harlem Renaissance may be found at: http://www.readwritethink.org/lessons/lesson_view.asp?id=252. If possible, invite a dance teacher to teach students and their families the swing and other popular dances of the time.

Satire

Satire is a literary form that criticizes humanity or institutions with sarcasm, wit, and humor for the purpose of showing their absurdity and need for improvement.

"Much to his surprise, Eugene was the lucky winner of an all-expenses-paid cruise to Bermuda. 'Terrific,' he said. 'I'll probably get a really nasty sunburn.'"

from *Terrific* by Jon Agee

✳ ✳ ✳

Selected Literature

Terrific written and illustrated by Jon Agee, 2005, Hyperion

After winning a trip to Bermuda, Eugene is shipwrecked on a deserted island with Lenny, the parrot. Using his sarcastic sense of humor, Eugene responds "TERRIFIC!" in each dire situation. The book also ridicules human beings by making the parrot in the book smarter than all the people.

Other Possible Literature Selections

An Undone Fairy Tale by Ian Lendler, illustrated by Whitney Martin, 2005, Simon & Schuster

Satirizing the avid reader and fairy tales, Ian Lendler creates an "unfinished fairy tale" in which a courageous knight wears a tutu and rides a fish on his quest to slay the dragon.

A Story with Pictures by Barbara Kanninen, illustrated by Lynn Rowe Reed, 2007, Holiday House

When an author forgets to give her manuscript to the illustrator, the artist paints whatever she imagines and makes the author and a crazed duck characters in her story. The absurdity of illustrating a book without the manuscript satirizes the illustrator, the writer, and the process of creating a picture book.

Lesson Idea

Collect four or five political cartoons or cartoon strips that use satire. The following Web site can assist you with your search: http://editorialcartoonists.com/cartoon/.

Make overhead transparencies of each cartoon. Display the cartoons, and ask students to identify what the cartoonist is making fun of or ridiculing. For example, a picture of a person standing in front of a gas pump with his pockets turned inside out while a CEO from an oil company counts piles of money in the background shows the absurdity of high gas prices and suggests that oil companies are making huge profits at the average citizen's expense. In addition to discussing what each cartoon or comic strip is ridiculing, have students note some of the techniques cartoonists use, such as hyperbole, sarcasm, and irony.

After the discussion, explain that when cartoonists or writers use humor to criticize, mock, or ridicule human beings or institutions, they are using satire. On the board, write the definition for satire. Ask students to think of other examples of cartoons, movies, commercials, or stories that use satire and share these with the class.

MATERIALS

☐ a variety of cartoons: political cartoons, comic books, comic strips, and editorial cartoons

☐ how-to books on drawing cartoons

☐ transparency of satiric techniques, p. 43

☐ material to make prize ribbons

Before, During, and After Reading

Before reading *Terrific* by Jon Agee aloud, explain that cartoonists and authors use specific techniques to create a satire. Make an overhead transparency of the techniques, definitions, and examples shown in the chart on page 43. Have students take notes on these satiric techniques or make copies for the class. Review each technique, definition, and example with students, and ask them to contribute additional examples. Tell students that there are other satiric techniques too, but these are the primary ones found in *Terrific*.

Satiric Technique	Definition	Example
Exaggeration	Making someone or something larger than life	A caricature: a person's physical features are often enlarged.
Irony	The opposite of what is expected or intended	A family taking their dream cruise ends up shipwrecked on an unknown island.
Sarcasm	A remark that mocks or ridicules someone or something; often it is intended to cause pain	While watching a downpour, a girl says "What a lovely day."
Reversal	A change in the natural order of things	A child disciplines a parent; a student actually runs the class instead of the teacher.

Tell students to listen for elements of satire the author uses as they listen to you read *Terrific*. Stop after page 1. Ask students what technique is being used when Eugene says, "'Terrific! . . . I'll probably get a really nasty sunburn.'" After students identify sarcasm as the technique, ask them what kind of people the author is mocking here (pessimists or people who have negative attitudes). Help students realize that the author also ridicules contests and contest winners too, by ironically having a sour puss win one.

Continue reading to the bottom of page 3. Stop and ask students what techniques they observe, leading them to identify irony (everyone is rescued except Eugene); exaggeration (Eugene is alone but believes he will be eaten by cannibals); and sarcasm ("'Terrific, he said, 'I'll probably get devoured by sharks'").

Read to the bottom of page 10 and stop. Ask students how the author has used the satiric technique of reversal. Note that the parrot has more sense and intelligence than the human: the bird draws the blueprint of the boat and tells Eugene how to build it!

Remind students to listen for other examples of satiric techniques as you finish reading. Then have pairs give one example of each satiric technique from this portion of the text. Allow time for pairs to share their results with the class.

Writing Activity

Invite students to create an original satirical cartoon strip. Before students begin writing, tell them that they must decide what or whom they are going to mock or ridicule. As a class, brainstorm some possible topics for satire such as school lunches, over-reliance on cell phones, or the effect of too many activities on family life.

Before students start their drafts, encourage them to peruse comic books, comic strips, and editorial cartoons to gather ideas. In addition, provide resources that show students how to draw cartoon characters and caricatures. Ask if there are classroom cartooning "experts" who can provide tips for the other students.

When students feel comfortable with the activity, allow them to work individually or with a partner to construct their original cartoon. Remind students to incorporate satiric techniques such as exaggeration, irony, and sarcasm in their cartoons.

After students draft, revise, edit, and produce the final copy of the cartoons, post their work around the classroom. Use sticky notes to number each cartoon. Then have students go on a gallery tour of the posted cartoons. After students return to their seats, ask them to vote for the cartoon that has the most original example of satire. Collect the ballots and award ribbons to the winning comic strips.

(LESSON EXTENSIONS)

✛ Challenge students to create satires of television commercials such as the Dr. Scholl gel foot insert ad, and perform them for the class.

✛ Suggest that students design a travel brochure or postcard that uses satire to advertise the ideal vacation spot such as the Black Lagoon.

Parody

> **Parody** is a humorous imitation of another literary work that is designed to entertain and poke fun at the original work's style or subject matter.

"'Oh, Romeow, where is that fur-faced Romeow?
I do not care that you are a cat or a Felini.
If you were a creature of any other name.
It would still make my tail wag.'"

from *Romeow and Drooliet* by Nina Laden

✳ ✳ ✳

Selected Literature

Romeow and Drooliet written and illustrated by Nina Laden, 2005, Chronicle Books

A story of love between Romeow the cat and Drooliet the dog is inspired by Shakespeare's tale of Romeo and Juliet but has a happier ending.

Other Possible Literature Selections

Three Silly Billies by Margie Palatini, illustrated by Barry Moser, 2005, Simon & Schuster

Three billy goats, unable to cross a bridge because they cannot pay the toll, form a car pool with The Three Bears, Little Red Riding Hood, and Jack, of beanstalk fame, to get past the rude Troll.

The Gingerbread Cowboy by Janet Squires, illustrated by Holly Berry, 2006, Laura Geringer Books

In this Western retelling of a classic tale, the Gingerbread Cowboy encounters a horned lizard, javelinas, and a herd of long-horned cattle as he "giddy ups" as fast as he can to escape from the rancher and his wife. Ultimately he is outwitted by a wily coyote.

Lesson Idea

Activate students' background knowledge by using a Think-Pair-Share strategy.

Ask the class to think about what they already know about Romeo and Juliet. Invite students to share their ideas with a partner. Explain to students that they will use their ideas for today's lesson about parody.

Show a brief clip of the ballroom scene from the 1968 movie *Romeo and Juliet* starring Leonard Whiting and Olivia Hussey and directed by Franco Zefferelli. Then ask students to quick write their thoughts and observations about this scene.

MATERIALS

❒ video clip of the ballroom scene from *Romeo and Juliet*, directed by Franco Zefferelli

❒ computer, VCR, or DVD player

❒ T-chart, p. 46

❒ Parody Story Writing Map, p. 47

❒ a variety of folk/fairy tale picture books

❒ How to Write a Readers Theater Script, p. 49

Before, During, and After Reading

Show students the cover of *Romeow and Drooliet*. Explain that as they listen to the story, they are to compare its text to what they already know and what they watched in the movie clip.

After reading aloud the story, invite students to complete a T-chart like the one below to compare and contrast the movie with the book.

My Observations of the Ballroom Scene From the Movie	My Observations of the Ballroom Scene From *Romeow and Drooliet*

Since the book is a humorous imitation of Shakespeare's tale of Romeo and Juliet, ask students to consider the following questions:

How does the book Romeow and Drooliet *make fun of the original version?*

Can you define and give an example of parody from the ball scene? (Show the students the picture of the ball scene in the book one more time.)

Have students share and discuss their comparisons with the entire class. Then create a whole-class definition of parody. Post it on a Literary Elements Word Wall.

Writing Activity

Use this lesson idea as a springboard for a writing activity. Divide the class into small groups of three or four, and challenge each group to create a parody of a fairy tale or folktale. Here are some suggestions to guide the parody-writing project:

◆ Create a folk/fairy tale classroom text set for your classroom library. Provide students with plenty of examples of both original tales and fractured fairy tales.

◆ Provide adequate browsing time and discussion time to talk about the features of the original tales.

◆ Encourage students to think about a specific tale and to decide how they will offer a humorous spin.

◆ Provide group reading and writing time throughout the writing process.

◆ Create a graphic organizer like the one shown below to guide students in their thinking and planning. Use *Romeow and Drooliet* to model how to complete it.

◆ Have groups work together to complete the writing map before they individually draft their parodies. Regroup them for peer editing and publishing.

PARODY STORY WRITING MAP		
Story Element	**Original or Close-to-Original Version of Tale**	**Parody**
Setting		
Time and Place		
Characters		
Problem		
Event 1		
Event 2		
Event 3		
Solution		

(LESSON EXTENSION)

✚ Invite students to create Readers Theater scripts of their parody. Readers Theater is a wonderful way of sharing stories, poems, or parts of plays and novels with others. It is also a proven instructional model to build reading fluency (Rasinski, 2003; Scraper, 2006). Readers use scripts, suggested characterization, and limited action and settings to bring the story to life.

Have students use the Parody Story Writing Map on page 47 to organize their thoughts for this activity. They may elect to use simple costumes, props, lighting effects, or music to create a mood, but this is entirely optional and depends on your time and resources. Additionally, you might wish to provide time for them to practice performing the script for an audience.

The scripts can also be used to review the concept of parody. Distribute copies of the students' scripts to the class. Provide highlighters and explain to students that their challenge is to read the script and locate the lines that show the tale is being parodied.

A direction sheet to guide students through the process of writing the script appears on page 49. Post these in the classroom or provide students with copies.

How to Write a Readers Theater Script

1. Think about the story you would like to perform for others. Read original versions of the tale and think about how you could create a parody of it.

2. Use a Parody Story Writing Map to help organize your thoughts. Think about the setting, characters, plot, problem, and solution.

3. Work with group members to create your script.

4. Decide how many characters and narrators you'll need.

5. Include dialogue and some action. Be sure to include stage directions such as "creeping through the forest" or "then the cows moo."

6. After the group finishes its first draft, peer edit your script before submitting it to your teacher.

7. After receiving your teacher's feedback, your group is ready to type the final script. Remember to follow the Readers Theater script format.

8. After making multiple copies of your final script, everyone in the group will use highlighters to mark the dialogue for each character's parts. Hint: It's a good idea to use different-colored highlighters to help actors and narrators distinguish their parts. You may have more than one narrator or you may decide to share the narrator role.

9. Practice your script. You'll want to rehearse the script several times. Be sure to speak clearly and to read the words loudly enough to be heard.

10. Discuss with your teacher whether you want to use simple props (i.e., a chair or a desk) and costumes. If you are playing music in the background to create a mood, be sure to bring in the necessary materials for practice and for the performance.

11. Decide on the day of the parody performance, and create flyers to share with other students, teachers, and parents for the big day. Be sure to borrow a digital camera to take lots of pictures of the performance. After the performance, ask the audience if they recognize the parody in these tales.

Teaching Literary Elements With Picture Books © 2009 by Susan Van Zile and Mary Napoli, Scholastic Teaching Resources

Point of View

> **Point of view** is the perspective from which a story is told. For fiction, the three most common points of view are first person, third-person limited, and third-person omniscient. For nonfiction, the third-person objective point of view is often used.

"'I was in my office eating some aphid lo mein when the phone buzzed. I answered it.'"

from *Ace Lacewing: Bug Detective* by David Biedrzycki

✳ ✳ ✳

Selected Literature

Ace Lacewing: Bug Detective written and illustrated by David Biedrzycki, 2005, Charlesbridge

Motham City is abuzz with the horrific news: Queenie Bee has been kidnapped! Determined to find the culprit, Ace Lacewing, Bug Detective, follows "a suspicious trail of honey," encountering numerous suspects and red herrings along the way. Told from the first-person point of view, this pun-filled story has a clever surprise ending that underscores the super sleuth's talent.

Other Literature Selections

Sophie's Masterpiece by Eileen Spinelli, illustrated by Jane Dyer, 2001, Simon and Schuster

Most residents at Beekman's Boardinghouse shun Sophie the spider's artistic creations except for a young expectant mother. For the new baby, Sophie lovingly weaves her masterpiece, leaving behind a piece of her heart and the reader's too. The story uses the third-person limited point of view.

George vs. George: The American Revolution as Seen from Both Sides by Rosalyn Schanzer, 2004, National Geographic

This nonfiction work considers both the American and British perspectives of the American Revolution as seen through the eyes of George Washington and King George III and uses the third-person objective point of view.

Lesson Idea

To introduce students to point of view, begin with a discussion of how a parent and a child might view the issue of raising the child's allowance. First have students do a quick write about the issue from the parent's perspective. Provide time for them to share their responses. Next have students do a quick write about the issue from the child's perspective and then share those responses. As a class, discuss the term *point of view*. Guide students in writing a definition on chart paper and post it.

Make an overhead transparency of examples of first- and third-person points of view like the ones below. For younger or struggling students, use the examples for first person and third-person limited point of view only.

MATERIALS

❏ overhead transparency of examples of different points of view

❏ 3–4 books representing different points of view

REPRODUCIBLES

Students
❏ Detective Story Graphic Organizer, p.75

◆ FIRST-PERSON POINT OF VIEW
One of the characters tells the story, using the pronoun *I*.

EXAMPLE: *I went to the store. Jessica went with me. We bought lots of spicy chips. I ate too many and got sick.*

◆ THIRD-PERSON LIMITED POINT OF VIEW
A story is told through the eyes of a single character using third person pronouns, such as *he* and *she*. In the example below, the point of view is limited because the reader only sees the event from Tommy's perspective.

EXAMPLE: *Tommy went to the store. Jessica, the girl on whom Tommy had a crush, went with him. They bought lots of spicy chips. He ate too many and got sick. Tommy felt really embarrassed.*

◆ **THIRD-PERSON OMNISCIENT POINT OF VIEW:**

Someone outside the story is observing the characters and events and reporting what can be seen and heard. This all-knowing narrator can see into the hearts and minds of all the characters and shows what they think and feel.

EXAMPLE: *Tommy went to the store thinking about how hungry he was. Jessica, the girl on whom he had a crush, went with him. Jessica had no idea how Tommy felt about her, but she thought he was cute. They bought some spicy chips. Tommy got sick and felt extremely embarrassed. Disgusted, Jessica walked home by herself.*

◆ **THIRD-PERSON OBJECTIVE POINT OF VIEW:**

A story or event is related by someone who is not involved and who reports only what can be seen and heard. It does *not* show what the characters think and feel. Often this point of view is used in newspaper articles, textbooks, and other works of nonfiction.

EXAMPLE: *Tommy went to the store. Jessica went with him. They bought lots of spicy chips. Tommy got sick. Jessica left.*

(Note: All italicized examples were provided by Wally Vogelsong and are used with permission.)

On the overhead, reveal one example at a time and ask the class who is telling the story. After sharing each example, write class definitions for each point of view represented on chart paper. Discuss the differences among the various examples.

Before, During, and After Reading

In their journals or on sheets of notebook paper, have students construct a 3-column chart with the following headings: **Book Title**, **Point of View**, **How I Know**.

Use an excerpt similar to the one below from *Sophie's Masterpiece* by Eileen Spinelli to model how to think about point of view and how to fill in the chart:

"Sophie knew when she wasn't wanted. She scampered across the wall and up the stairs into the tugboat captain's closet."

After reading aloud the passage say: *This is the third person limited point of view. I know this because the pronoun* she *is used, which shows someone outside the story is telling it. The line "Sophie knew when she wasn't wanted" indicates that the reader sees events from Sophie's perspective.*

Again, as you model, complete the chart. Your finished product might look something like this:

Book Title	Point of View	How I Know
Sophie's Masterpiece	3rd-person limited	• Uses pronoun <u>she</u> • Only know what Sophie thinks—"she wasn't wanted"

To reinforce the concept of point of view, read three or four passages from various books that represent different points of view. After reading each example, stop and provide time for pairs of students to list the point of view and reasons for their choice on their chart. Discuss their responses and clarify any misconceptions.

Read the opening of *Ace Lacewing: Bug Detective* on page 4, and then stop. Ask students to predict what point of view is being used. Continue reading through page 6, and then stop. Have students confirm or revise their prediction based on evidence in the text. Before you finish reading the book, tell students to think about the impact point of view has on the story.

After reading, have the class evaluate the point of view: Was it effective? Why or why not? How would the story differ if Queen Bee had told it? How would the story change if it were written from the third-person point of view?

Writing Activity

Have students use first-person point of view to create a detective story. Use *Ace Lacewing: Bug Detective* to model the elements to include in a detective story. On chart paper, construct a chart similar to the one on page 54 and fill in the story elements.

Direct individuals or pairs to complete the Detective Story Graphic Organizer and then write a draft, peer edit, revise, and publish their story. Provide time for students to share their work in small groups. Have each group select one story to share with the class. To display students' work, create a bulletin board titled "Ace Detective Stories."

Detective Story Elements	Ace Lacewing Bug Detective
Point of View	1st person
Setting (time and place)	1920's–1930's, Motham City
Detective	Ace Lacewing
Victim	Queenie Bee
Suspects	Roaches, Cicada, Twig, Smooch
Witnesses	Maggot, the drone-who-knows-the-truth
Criminal/Motive	Princess Pollen; jealousy, desire for power
Crime	Kidnapping
Clues	Trail of honey; victim's location revealed by the-drone-who-knows-the-truth; stench of pollen from "Al the Drone"
Obstacles/Stumbling Blocks/ Red Herrings	Blind maggot's testimony; drive-by-gassing of the-drone-that-knows-the-truth; Ace and Zito being captured
Solution	Xerces and the police arrive and arrest Princess Pollen and her accomplices.

(LESSON EXTENSIONS)

✚ Have students use the first-person point of view to retell *Ace Lacewing: Bug Detective* from Queenie Bee's, Princess Pollen's, or another character's perspective.

✚ After reading aloud pages 18–26 of *George vs. George, The American Revolution as Seen from Both Sides*, divide the class in half. One half will be George Washington. The other half will be King George III. Tell the George Washington side to use first-person point of view to write a letter to King George to convince him to open Boston Harbor and stop taxation without representation. Challenge students to give at least three reasons for King George to change Britain's stand on tea and taxes, and have them use evidence from the text to support their ideas.

Conversely, tell the King George III side to use first-person point of view to write a letter to George Washington to convince him to purchase tea from Great Britain and to pay British taxes. Challenge this group to provide at least three reasons for George Washington to change the colonies stand on tea and taxes, using evidence from the text to support their ideas. Then pair students from each side, and have them read their letters to one another.

Voice

Voice refers to the way an author speaks to readers to show his or her feelings or attitude toward the subject. Voice makes the reader feel emotions. It is "confidence, enthusiasm, personality, and individual expressiveness" (Spandel, 2001, p. 61).

"'THIS IS IT! The picture that's going to get me my first front page. A real-life vampire exposed! The editor is going to <u>love</u> it!'"

from *Scoop! An Exclusive by Monty Molenski* written and illustrated
by John Kelly and Cathy Tincknell

✳ ✳ ✳

Selected Literature

Scoop: An Exclusive by Monty Molenski, written and illustrated by John Kelly and Cathy Tincknell, 2007, Candlewick Press

Always searching for the sensational story yet inevitably and ironically missing the big picture, Monty Molenski follows his coworkers to uncover the mystery of clandestine meetings at the F. P. Club. While on his hilarious mission, Molenski accidentally captures the real scoop with his "broken" camera.

Other Possible Literature Selections

Sweet Tooth by Margie Palatini, illustrated by Jack E. Davis, 2004, Simon & Schuster

Stewart's demanding, talking sweet tooth runs and ruins his life, causing the boy to do outrageous things like stuff wedding cake into his mouth before the bride and groom cut it. The bold type and capitalizations clearly allow the reader to hear the voice of this cantankerous inanimate object.

My Light written and illustrated by Molly Bang, 2004, Blue Sky Press

In this beautifully illustrated book, the sun tells its story of light, explaining the process of how its energy is used to enhance life and generate electricity.

Lesson Idea

. . . .

To introduce voice, have students take turns saying an innocuous phrase or sentence such as "How are you today?" or "I'm fine" in a variety of voices and tones ranging from cheerful to angry. Ask what feeling or emotion the speaker's tone conveys to the listener. Explain that authors convey feelings and emotions in their writing just as we do when we speak. Then define the term *voice*.

MATERIALS

☐ newspapers, including tabloids

☐ clothesline, clothes pins, balloons, streamers (optional)

REPRODUCIBLES

Students

☐ Front Page News Graphic Organizer, p.76

Before, During, and After Reading

Before reading *Scoop!* project images of pages 1 and 2 on a visualizer (document camera) or provide small groups with a copy of the text. Have students identify all the following voices depicted on the page:

◆ Molenski's (see his note titled "This is it!"; the ID badge; reminders, and journal)
◆ the boss's (see his note)
◆ secretary's (see her message)
◆ camera repairman's (see his words on the repair bill)

Discuss the feelings or emotions each voice conveys. Ask: *What do the voices reveal about the personality of the characters?* On the board or chart paper, list students' responses in a chart similar to the one below.

Character's Name	Voice	Traits Voice Reveals
Molenski	excited, annoyed, passionate, determined	wants to be ACE reporter; obsessed with supernatural; forgetful
The boss	outraged	angry with Molenski
Len	seems puzzled	overcharges customers; incompetent
The secretary	alarmed	emotional; efficient

Point out that even the details in the text—the titles of the books (*Top Ten Conspiracy Theories*, *Space Cadets*, and so on) and the images on the film strip—show how passionate Molenski is about the supernatural and underscore the enthusiasm and excitement in his voice.

After reading aloud pages 3 and 4, stop and ask students to describe Molenski's voice and then the boss's. Encourage them to describe the voice conveyed in the front page headline. On pages 5 and 6 have students analyze Chris Croc's voice. Continue the process of dramatically reading aloud the text and stopping to discuss new voices or changes in Molenski's voice. Don't forget to focus on the various voices in the real and imagined headlines. Note the voices of the protesting spirits—"Stop the Séances" (pages 1–14). Observe the changes in print size and capitalization. For example, THE MYSTERY IS ABOUT TO BE SOLVED! (page 22) and "Oh dear!" represent two very different voices. Discuss the changes in Molenski's voice at the end of the story as conveyed in his Monday-through-Friday journal entries.

Writing Activity

Have students create sensational characters and events to create a tabloid-style front page news story—using the voice of an ACE reporter like Molenski. As a class, brainstorm a list of potential topics. Consider having students use the topics suggested by Molenski's award-winning front pages. Let the front page illustrations in the text and school-appropriate front pages from popular tabloids generate more writing ideas.

After students chose a topic, pair them. Have partners role play and conduct interviews with such characters as Big Foot, a mummy, an alien, the living Elvis, the Loch Ness monster, ghosts, and other sensational characters. Remind students to interview eyewitnesses as well; partners will role play these characters too. As students interview and role play, they should take notes and record relevant dialogue to use in their article.

Following the interviews, pass out front page news articles for students to read and discuss the format for writing a news article (headlines, by-lines, datelines, and so on). Also talk about the inverted pyramid organizational structure that most news articles use: The most important facts appear first and the article ends with the least important facts. Remind students to begin with the 5 W's and H (Who, What, Where, When, Why, and How) to relate the most important facts.

Distribute the Front Page News Graphic Organizer, and have students complete it before drafting their article. As they draft, remind them to use the voice of a tabloid reporter and to give the sensational characters and eyewitnesses distinct voices as well. Then allow time for them to peer edit and revise.

To publish the articles, students can use the computer or large sheets of newsprint to create a tabloid-style front page that capitalizes on their news article. They can also use photographs, clip art, original drawings, and various fonts or lettering styles to customize their front page and make it look authentic. In addition, the featured news articles can be typed in the newspaper format of columns.

In the auditorium or classroom, set up a Front Page Club, similar to the one illustrated in the book. Use a clothesline and clothes pins to hang students' work around the room, and decorate the room with balloons and streamers. Appoint an outside Master of Ceremonies, such as the principal, to present awards Like "Most Sensational Headline" or "Best Story" to students.

(LESSON EXTENSION)

✚ Use *Sweet Tooth* as a model and have students write a dialogue between a person and his disobedient body part.

Word Choice

> **Word choice** concerns using specific language to help the reader get a picture in his or her head. Rebecca Olness defines it as "the precision in the use of the words—word smithery" (2005, p. 115).

"'The moon,' [Selig] wrote in his notebook, growing more and more excited with each word, 'melted like a *lemon lozenge* in the licorice sky.'"

from *The Boy Who Loved Words* by Roni Schotter

✳ ✳ ✳

Selected Literature

The Boy Who Loved Words by Roni Schotter, illustrated by Gissell Potter, 2006, Random House

Selig passionately collects words. When he discovers his bulging pockets can no longer hold them all, Selig goes on a quest to discover his purpose and learns he can provide the perfect word for everyone who needs one.

Other Possible Literature Selections

Beauty and the Beaks: A Turkey's Cautionary Tale by Mary Jane Auch and Herm Auch, 2006, Holiday House

Lance, the pompous turkey, arrives at the Chic Hen beauty salon and brags about being invited to a special feast. When Beauty discovers Lance is the main course for this "eggsclusive" event, she and the other hens give him "an eggstreme makeover" to save the day.

Fancy Nancy by Jane O'Connor, illustrated by Robin Preiss Glasser, 2006, HarperCollins

Vivacious, ebullient Nancy teaches her family how to be fancy as she splashes extraordinary words across the page in this delightful story about familial love.

Lesson Idea

Before reading aloud *The Boy Who Loved Words*, create the following cloze passage from the first page of the text. Model the process of filling in the blanks in the first paragraph for students, but do not use the words from the text. Then have them complete the remaining paragraphs.

MATERIALS

❐ copies of the cloze passage for *The Boy Who Loved Words*, p. 60

❐ overhead transparency of the first 3 paragraphs on page 3 of *The Boy Who Loved Words* (answer key for first paragraph of cloze passage)

❐ strips of Velcro®

Cloze Passage for *The Boy Who Loved Words*

Selig _____ everything about words—the sound of them in his ears (tintinnabulating!), the taste of them on his tongue _____, the thought of them when they _____ in his brain (stirring!), and, most especially, the feel of them when they moved his heart (Mama!).

Whenever Selig heard a word he liked, he'd _____ it loud, _____ it down on a piece of paper, then _____ it into his pocket to save. Such a collector!

Selig's pockets positively _____ with words. He stuffed new ones inside his _____, down his _____, up his _____, under his _____.

On an overhead projector, show the first, second, and third paragraphs on page 2 of *The Boy Who Loved Words*. Have students compare your word choices and theirs to the author's and discuss similarities and differences. For example, if students write, "Whenever Selig heard a word he liked, he'd <u>say</u> it loud, <u>write</u> it down on a piece of paper, then <u>put</u> it into his pocket to save," note the differences between *say* and *shout*, *write* and *jot*, and so on. Guide students to discover that using precise words, particularly specific nouns and verbs, helps readers paint a vivid picture of the text in their mind.

Before, During, and After Reading

Before you begin reading, tell students to simply listen to the story to enjoy the mysterious new words and to think about what message the author is trying to convey about word choice. Emphasize the words in italics and explain that they're defined in the glossary at the back of the book.

After reading the story, discuss the key points the author makes about word choice and, on chart paper, create a class list of Helpful Hints to Develop Word Choice. If desired, use the list below as a guide. Tips 1–6 are ideas from the book and tips 7–10 are additional.

Helpful Hints to Develop Word Choice

1. Feel passionate about the words you use in a piece of writing.
2. Collect words and share your collection.
3. Use collected words precisely and in the right situation.
4. Discard words that do not fit the context.
5. Play with words and rearrange them until they sound just right.
6. Fit fancy words naturally into writing and use them sparingly.
7. Choose words that appeal to your audience.
8. Observe unusual word choices in the books you read, such as hyphenated adjectives or invented words, and try using them in your own work.
9. Try using various literary devices in your writing such as onomatopoeia, similes, metaphors, imagery, hyperbole, and alliteration.
10. Reread drafts and revise them to replace nouns and verbs with stronger ones.

Have Fun With Words!

Writing Activity

Using words from *The Boy Who Loved Words*, create a classroom word tree. Make a large tree out of butcher paper, laminate it, and hang it on the wall. Give an index card with a different word from the text to each student. Have students refer to the glossary to write the definition of their word on the back of the card and then teach the word to the rest of the class. Velcro® the words to the word tree. Encourage students to collect new words from their own reading to add to the tree.

Then ask students to use five words from the word tree to create a brief vignette that portrays a situation in which the words make a difference in someone's life. As a model, use the example of the baker whose business is transformed from mediocre to booming because of Selig's words. Revisit this section of the text (page 24) and have students find the words that help sell the baked goods.

(LESSON EXTENSIONS)

✚ Have students invent a product and use some of Selig's words to sell it. Suggest that they use the words on the word tree in their ads. After students peer edit, revise, and publish their ads, consider having an employee from a local advertising agency come in to judge the ads and award prizes for them.

✚ In response to *Beauty and the Beaks: A Turkey's Cautionary Tale*, have students compose chicken jokes or puns. Use the following example below as a model:

"'My life is about to eggspire!' blubbered Lance.

'Don't chicken out now,' said Beauty. 'We'll hide you.'

'Are you yolking?' squawked Gladys. 'He's too big to hide.'"

✚ Have students go on a scavenger hunt to search for vivid verbs in *Beauty and the Beaks: A Turkey's Cautionary Tale*. Award a prize to the student who collects the most verbs. After discussing the importance of using vivid verbs in writing with the class, have students revise the verbs in one of their drafts. A similar activity can be used to help students use more exact nouns.

✚ Point out the specialized beauty salon vocabulary the authors use in *Beauty and the Beaks* (*trim, color, touch-up, set, comb-out, pedicure*) and state that using specialized vocabulary lends authenticity to the work. Ask students to think about a hobby or a pastime they enjoy, such as skateboarding, cheerleading, or playing soccer, and have them make a list of specialized vocabulary associated with the activity. Then challenge them to use this specialized vocabulary to write a rap, poem, or how-to paragraph about the activity.

Style

> **Style** refers to the author's personality on paper, including his or her use of unique writing techniques.

wide roads
side roads
perfect-for-a-ride roads
rough roads
tough roads
just-can't-get-enough roads

From *Motorcycle Song* by Diane Siebert

✳ ✳ ✳

Selected Literature

Motorcycle Song by Diane Siebert, illustrated by Leonard Jenkins, 2002, HarperCollins

The author takes the reader on a poetic motorcycle journey down country roads and city streets, vividly describing the song of the motorcycle as it vrooms, purrs, and roars along.

Other Possible Literature Selections

The Recess Queen by Alexis O'Neill, illustrated by Laura Huliska-Beith, 2002, Scholastic Press

As invented words and vivid verbs splash across the pages, Mean Jean the Recess Queen is trumped by teeny, tiny Katy Sue, the new kid who fights back and ultimately befriends the playground bully.

Mr. George Baker by Amy Hest, illustrated by Jon J. Muth, 2004, Candlewick Press

One-hundred-year-old Mr. George Baker waits for the school bus each day beside his friend and first-grade neighbor, the narrator, who brilliantly describes George's "crookedy fingers" going "tappidy-boom" across his knees. Both characters support each other as they learn how to read in this tender, heart-warming tale.

Lesson Idea

● ● ● ● ● ● ● ● ● ● ● ● ●

To introduce style, play a variety of music including opera, jazz, country, and pop rock. Explain that what differentiates these musical compositions from one another is their style— the way the notes are arranged, played, and sung. Ask students to describe the style of some of the musical pieces. Consider using a chart similar to the one below to record students' responses.

Opera	Jazz	Country	Pop Rock
emotional	soulful	feet-stomping	electric

Point out that while musical styles depend primarily on the arrangement of notes, writing styles depend on the arrangement of words. Because of the way authors express themselves on paper through word choice, syntax (the way the words and phrases are arranged), and voice, writing styles can be as varied as musical compositions.

Before, During, and After Reading

Before reading *Motorcycle Song*, use a visualizer, overhead projector, or multiple copies of the text to display the words on the first page. Read the page out loud. Discuss what students notice about the author's style and list their observations on chart paper. As necessary, guide them to notice the rhyme scheme, variation in line length, absence of capital letters, vivid verbs, hyphenated adjectives, repetition, and emphasis on *-ing* word endings. Ask students what the author's style shows about the motorcycle guy's attitude toward his machine and riding. What does the author's attitude toward her subject appear to be?

Repeat the same procedure with the second page of text. During the discussion about the author's style, direct students' attention to the chart paper to see which

MATERIALS

❏ a variety of fashion magazines (optional)

❏ Scaffold organizer, p. 65

techniques Diane Siebert repeats. Add new observations to the list.

Read pages 5–9, stopping at the end of the description of the roads. On the chart, record observations students make about the roads' description. Continue reading in meaningful chunks, pausing to discuss Siebert's style after the descriptions of the bikers, the bikes, the motorcycle guy heading toward gas and food, the bikers eating and chatting, and the rider's journey back to town.

Writing Activity

Invite students to choose a mode of transportation with which they are familiar, such as a bike, skateboard, scooter, car, bus, truck, boat, or plane. Then, using the text's description of the "bikes" on page 18 as a model for writing, have students imitate the author's style as they describe their selected mode of transportation by completing a Scaffold Organizer similar to the one below. To use the scaffold effectively, students must view Siebert's text simultaneously. Show the selection on page 18 on the overhead or on a visualizer. If possible, provide students with multiple copies of the text to view.

_____ Song
by _____

_____ _____
_____ _____
_____ _____ _____
_____ _____
_____ _____
_____ _____ _____

_____ that _____
_____ that _____
_____ that _____ _____ _____ _____ _____

_____ that _____
and
_____ that _____

_____
_____
_____
_____
_____ or _____
_____ _____ and _____ _____

After peer editing and revising the draft of their "style" poems, students can cut out a large construction paper silhouette of their bus, car, skateboard, or other mode of transportation and then glue the poem to it. Display the final products on the classroom bulletin board.

(LESSON EXTENSIONS)

✚ Use *The Recess Queen* as a springboard for creating jump rope raps that include invented words, words that vary in size and shape, rhyme, repetition, and other elements of the author's style.

✚ Collect pictures from various fashion magazines that reflect a variety of clothing styles from casual to formal. In class, share a well-written fashion feature article. After reading the article, discuss its style and generate a list of a fashion article's unique features. Afterward form small groups. Distribute one picture of a model to each group and tell groups not to show the picture to other students. Using the voice and style of a fashion reviewer or a fashion show commentator, have groups compose a description of the outfit the model is wearing. When the groups are finished writing, collect the pictures, mix them up, and hang each one on the board. As a group shares its description, have the rest of the class identify the picture being described. If desired, award bonus points or small prizes to students who correctly match the picture to its description.

Appendix

Teacher's Script for Memoir-Nudging Questions

Before students draw a picture of their memory, have them close their eyes and visualize the event. Ask them "nudging questions" to help them "see." If using the script below, read the questions slowly in a quiet, soothing voice. Softly play a piece of relaxing music such as Vivaldi's *Four Seasons* in the background. After the visualization, tell students to draw a picture of their memory. Then go on a partner walk and talk where pairs converse about the events they have chosen for their topic. As students talk, encourage them to ask each other questions about the incident or event to bring it to life. Model this questioning strategy before going on the walk. This process enhances even the reluctant writer's fluency.

Nudging Questions for Memoir or Personal Narrative

◆ Visualize the memory about which you have chosen to write. Where are you? Are you inside or outside? In the city? Country? Suburbs? Abroad? At home? At school? Visiting a friend or relative?

◆ What time of day is it? Is it light or dark, dawn or midday? What is the season? Are you burning and sweating under the sweltering sun, or are snowflakes gently brushing your cheeks? Is a light spring breeze blowing, or are you frolicking in the fall leaves?

◆ Where in this place are you located? What do you see from this place? What objects surround you? Are they natural or human-made? What colors stand out? Is anyone with you? A person? An animal? What do they look like? How are they dressed? What kinds of expressions appear on their faces? How do they move? What gestures do you notice? Slowly move your mind's eye from left to right and focus on each object, person, or animal in your memory.

◆ As you begin writing about your memory, think about what sensory experiences you associate with this place. For instance, what do you smell? What odors or aromas stand out?

What do you feel in this place? Imagine that you are touching the objects. What textures can you sense?

What do you hear in this memory place? Listen to the sounds around you. Do you hear voices? If you are outdoors, what sounds are the weather, city, or animals producing?

What do you taste in this memory place? As you consider this question, think beyond food to sensory experiences in the environment as well. For example, if you are hiking, can you taste dust from a bone-dry hiking trail? If you are crying, can you taste the briny salt of tears?

Teaching Literary Elements With Picture Books © 2009 by Susan Van Zile and Mary Napoli, Scholastic Teaching Resources

Name _____ Date _____

Memoir Map

Memoir Topic _____

Who is involved in the event or experience?

_____

_____

_____

_____

Where and **when** does the event take place?

_____

What I saw, heard, smelled, tasted or touched:

_____

Event One

WHAT HAPPENED?

Event Two

Event Three

Event Four

Teaching Literary Elements With Picture Books © 2009 by Susan Van Zile and Mary Napoli, Scholastic Teaching Resources

Understanding Metaphors

Metaphor	What two things are being compared?	How are they alike?	What idea is the author trying to convey?

Teaching Literary Elements With Picture Books © 2009 by Susan Van Zile and Mary Napoli, Scholastic Teaching Resources

Name _____ Date _____

City Research Organizer

What is the city's origin?

What are some historical facts about the city?

City _____

What important events and people are associated with this city?

What are some of the city's interesting sights and unique characteristics or features?

Name _____ Date _____

City Character Profile

Name _____ Date of Birth _____

Background Information (origin and history) _____

_____

Eye Color _____ Hair Color/Style _____

Height _____ Weight _____ Build _____

Other Physical Traits (include unique features) _____

Enjoys wearing _____

List Five (5) Adjectives to Describe Its Personality:

_____

_____

Laughs Out Loud When _____

_____

Cries Inconsolably When _____

_____

Gets Embarrassed By _____

_____

Favorite Foods _____

Favorite Pastimes (sports, music) _____

Likes to Visit _____

Is Friends With (type of people the city attracts) _____

Dislikes _____

Important Achievements _____

Teaching Literary Elements With Picture Books © 2009 by Susan Van Zile and Mary Napoli, Scholastic Teaching Resources

Instantly Ironic

Setting _____
Time _____
Place _____

Characters:
Name _____ Description _____
Name _____ Description _____

Ironic Situation: What the character(s) expect to happen

_____
_____

Event 1

_____
_____

Event 2

_____
_____

Event 3

_____
_____

Ironic Outcome: The opposite of what the character(s) expects to happen

_____
_____

Writing With a Theme

Obstacle

_____
_____
_____

Failed Attempt

_____
_____
_____
_____

Feeling

_____
_____
_____

Failed Attempt

_____
_____
_____
_____

Feeling

_____
_____
_____

Failed Attempt

_____
_____
_____
_____

Feeling

_____
_____
_____

What I Learned/Theme

_____
_____
_____

Teaching Literary Elements With Picture Books © 2009 by Susan Van Zile and Mary Napoli, Scholastic Teaching Resources

Name _____ Date _____

Detective Story Graphic Organizer

What is the setting?

Time: _____

Place: _____

Who are the characters?

	Name(s)	Description(s)
Detective	_____	_____
Victim(s)	_____	_____
Suspect(s)	_____	_____
Witness(es)	_____	_____
Criminal(s)	_____	_____

What is the crime?

_____

_____

What are the clues?

_____

_____

What are the obstacles, stumbling blocks, or red herrings?

_____

_____

What is the solution?

_____

_____

Front Page News Graphic Organizer

_____
HEADLINE

WHO? _____
WHAT? _____
WHERE? _____
WHEN? _____

MOST IMPORTANT FACTS

WHY? _____
_____
HOW? _____
_____

LESS IMPORTANT FACTS

_____
_____
_____
_____

LEAST IMPORTANT FACTS

_____
_____
_____

Teaching Literary Elements With Picture Books © 2009 by Susan Van Zile and Mary Napoli, Scholastic Teaching Resources

Picture Books Cited

Agee, J. (2005). *Terrific*. New York: Hyperion.

Arnold, T. (2004). *Even more parts*. New York: Dial.

Auch, M. J., & Auch, H. (2006). *Beauty and the beaks: A turkey's cautionary tale*. New York: Holiday House.

Bang, M. (2004). *My light*. New York: Blue Sky Press.

Bee, W. (2005). *Whatever*. Cambridge, MA: Candlewick.

Biedrzycki, D. (2005). *Ace Lacewing: Bug detective*. Watertown, MA: Charlesbridge.

Bosak, S. (2004). *Dream: A tale of wonder, wisdom, & wishes*. Whitchurch-Stouffville, ON: TCP Press.

Burleigh, R. (2004). *Langston's train ride*. New York: Orchard.

Chall, M. W. (2003). *Prairie train*. New York: HarperCollins.

Edwards, W. (2004). *Monkey business*. Tonawanda, NY: Kids Can Press.

Fleischman, P. (1989). *Joyful noise: Poems for two voices*. New York: Harper Trophy.

Fletcher, R. (2003). *Hello, harvest moon*. New York: Clarion.

Giovanni, N. (2005). *Rosa*. New York: Henry Holt.

Heine, T. (2004). *Elephant dance: Memories of India*. Cambridge, MA: Barefoot Books.

Hest, A. (2004). *Mr. George Baker*. Cambridge, MA: Candlewick.

Johnson, D. A. (2006). *Snow sounds: An onomatopoeic story*. Boston: Houghton Mifflin.

Kanninen, B. (2007). *A story with pictures*. New York: Holiday House.

Kelley, T. (2005). *School lunch*. New York: Holiday House.

Kelly, J., & Tincknell, C. (2007). *Scoop: An exclusive by Monty Molenski*. Cambridge, MA: Candlewick.

Kimmel, E. A. (2000). *Grizz!* New York: Holiday House.

Kranking, K. W. (2003). *The ocean is . . .* New York: Henry Holt.

Laden, N. (2005). *Romeow and Drooliet*. San Francisco: Chronicle.

Laminack, L. (2004). *Saturday and teacakes*. Atlanta, GA: Peachtree Publishers.

Leedy, L., & Street, P. (2003). *There's a frog in my throat: 440 animal sayings a little bird told me*. New York: Holiday House.

Lendler, I. (2005). *An undone fairy tale*. New York: Simon & Schuster.

Merriam, E. (2004). "Metaphor." In L. B. Hopkins (Ed.), *Wonderful words: Poems about reading, writing, speaking, and listening*. New York: Simon & Schuster.

Michelson, R. (2006). *Across the alley*. New York: G. P. Putnam's Sons.

Miller, D. (2003). *Artic lights, Artic nights*. New York: Walker & Company.

Mora, P. (2005). *Dona Flor*. New York: Knopf.

Myers, C. (2005). *Lies and other tall tales*. New York: HarperCollins.

Nolen, J. (2003). *Thunder Rose*. San Diego, CA: Harcourt.

O'Connor. J. (2006). *Fancy Nancy*. New York: HarperCollins.

O'Neill, A. (2002). *The recess queen*. New York: Scholastic.

Oxenbury, H. (2005). *Pig tale*. New York: Margaret K. McElderry.

Palatini, M. (2004). *Sweet tooth*. New York: Simon & Schuster.

Palatini, M. (2005). *Three silly billies*. New York: Simon & Schuster.

Rappaport, D. (2005). *The school is not white! A true story of the Civil Rights movement*. New York: Hyperion.

Raschka, C. (2005). *New York is English, Chattanooga is Creek*. New York: Atheneum.

Rylant, C. (2000). *In November*. San Diego, CA: Harcourt.

Sams, C. R., & Stoick, J. (2000). *Stranger in the woods: A photographic fantasy*. Auburn Hills, MI: EDCO Publishing.

Schanzer, R. (2004). *George vs. George: The American Revolution as seen from both sides*. Westchester, NY: National Geographic.

Schotter, R. (2006). *The boy who loved words*. New York: Random House.

Shore, D. Z. & Alexander, J. (2006). *This is the dream*. New York: HarperCollins.

Siebert, D. (2002). *Motorcycle song*. New York: HarperCollins.

Siebert, D. (2000). *Cave*. New York: HarperCollins.

Spinelli, E. (2001). *Sophie's masterpiece*. New York: Simon and Schuster.

Squires, J. (2006). *The gingerbread cowboy*. New York: Laura Geringer.

Professional References

Beck, I. L., & McKeown, M. G. (1991). Conditions of vocabulary acquisition. In P.D. Pearson (Ed.), *The Handbook of Reading Research* (Vol. 2, pp. 780–814). New York: Longman.

Fletcher, R., & Portalupi, J. (1998). *Craft lessons: Teaching writing K–8*. Portland: Stenhouse.

Hall, S. (2002). *Using picture storybooks to teach literary devices* (Vol. 3). Westport, CT: Oryx Press.

Heard, G. (1999). *Awakening the heart: Exploring poetry in elementary and middle school*. Portsmouth: Heinemann. Lancia, P. (1997). Literary borrowing: The effects of literature in children's writing. *The Reading Teacher, 50*, 470–475.

Lynch-Brown, C., & Tomlinson, C. M. (2005). Essentials of children's literature (5th ed.). Boston: Allyn & Bacon.

Nagy, W. (1988). *Teaching vocabulary to improve comprehension*. Newark, NJ: International Reading Association.

Newkirk, T. (2004). *Misreading masculinity*. Portsmouth, NH: Heinemann.

Olness, R. (2005). *Using literature to enhance writing instruction*. Newark, NJ: International Reading Association.

Rasinski, T. (2003). *The Fluent reader: Oral reading strategies for building word recognition, fluency, and comprehension*. New York: Scholastic.

Robb, L. (2000). *Teaching reading in middle school: A strategic approach to teaching reading that improves comprehension and thinking*. New York: Scholastic.

Santa, C., Havens, L., & Valdes, B. (2004). *Project CRISS: Creating independence through student owned strategies* (3rd Ed.). Dubuque: Kendall/Hunt.

Schwartz, R. (1988). Learning to learn vocabulary in content area textbooks. *Journal of Reading, 32*, 108–118.

Schwartz, R., & Raphael, T. E. (1985). Concept of definition: A key to improving students' vocabulary. *The Reading Teacher, 39*, 198–205.

Scraper, K. (2006). *What a character! Bringing out the best in your students through reader's theatre*. Paper presented at International Reading Association, Chicago, IL. Retrieved October 19, 2007, from http://www.edwriter.com/downloads/2006_IRA_Handout.pdf

Serafini, F. (2007). Position statement: Using picture books with older readers. Retrieved June 3, 2008 from http://www.frankserafini.com/MainPages/posit-states.html.

Shanahan, T. (1990). Reading and writing together: What does it really mean? In T. Shanahan (Ed.), *Reading and writing together: New perspectives for the classroom* (pp. 1–18). Norwood, MA: Christopher-Gordon.

Spandel, V. (2001). *Creating writers through 6-trait writing assessment and instruction* (3rd ed.). New York: Longman.

Taylor, W. (1953). Cloze procedure: A new tool for measuring readability. *Journalism Quarterly, 30*, 415–433.

Wood Ray, K., & Laminack, L. (2001). *The writing workshop: Working through the hard parts (and they're all hard parts)*. Urbana, IL: National Council of Teachers of English.

Vacca, R., & Vacca, J. (2008). *Content area reading: Literacy and learning across the curriculum* (9th ed.). Boston: Pearson.

Web Resources for Information About Award-Winning Literature Selections

The following links provide information about award-winning books that pertain to language arts. These links can be accessed to find more books to use as models for writing:

1. The Children's Literature Assembly of the (NCTE) advocates the importance of utilizing literature for teaching children and young adults. Information about the Notable Books for Language Arts can be found on their Web site http://www.childrensliteratureassembly.org/index.htm

2. The Notable Books for a Global Society (NBGS) Committee, part of the International Reading Association Children's Literature and Reading Special Interest Group, selects each year a list of outstanding trade books for enhancing student understanding of people and cultures throughout the world. Winning titles include fiction, nonfiction, and poetry written for students in grades K–12. The winning titles each year are announced at the International Reading Association convention. You can access these titles by visiting the Web site http://www.tcnj.edu/~childlit/

3. Information about the Orbis Pictus Award, which recognizes excellence in the writing of nonfiction for children and young adults, may be found at http://www.ncte.org/elem/awards/orbispictus

4. The American Library Association (www.ala.org) honors illustrators and authors with numerous awards including the Caldecott Medal, Coretta Scott King Book Award, Belpré Award, and Siebert Medal.

5. The Lee Bennett Hopkins Poetry award is given to the best book of children's poetry published in the United States in the preceding year. The award is co-sponsored by Mr. Hopkins, the University Libraries, and the Pennsylvania Center for the Book. Information can be found at http://pabook.libraries.psu.edu/activities/hopkins/hopkins.html